EXPORT
for the
SMALL
BUSINESS

To
Jack Kailides MIEx
and his son
Nick Kailides, now
Principal, Central London College

EXPORT
for the
SMALL
BUSINESS

Second Edition

Henry Deschampsneufs

Kogan Page

Acknowledgements

The author thanks the following organisations for kind permission to reproduce copyright material: the Bank Education Service, British Airways, the London Chamber of Commerce and Industry, SITPRO, Union Transport (London) Ltd and Witherby & Co Ltd. Illustration 7.9 is Crown copyright and reproduced with the permission of the Controller of Her Majesty's Stationery Office.

First published in 1984
Second edition 1988
Reprinted with revisions 1990

Kogan Page Limited
120 Pentonville Road
London N1 9JN

British Library Cataloguing in Publication Data

A CIP record for this book is available from the British Library.

ISBN 1 85091 725 6

Printed and bound in Great Britain by
Biddles Ltd, Guildford and King's Lynn

Contents

List of Illustrations

Chapter 1

What's In It For Me?

No small business can properly afford to embark on any new activity until it is reasonably sure that adequate benefits will result. Moreover, it will have to be assured that involvement with customers overseas, which is what export is all about, will not be too demanding on the limited material, manpower and financial resources of the company. Before you contemplate exporting, therefore, you should know the answers to six key questions:

- ☐ Why should a small business export?
- ☐ What can you export?
- ☐ To whom should you export?
- ☐ How can the goods best be exported?
- ☐ How can you make money from export?
- ☐ How can you guard against failure?

This book attempts to answer these questions, so read it before taking the final decision whether or not to export.

Why should a small business export?

You must have good and sufficient reasons for adding export trade to your domestic business.

The time is right
There has probably never been a better time to become involved with export, for two main reasons.

First, there is a noticeable change taking place in international trade. For many years we have lived in a world of mass production, where the producers of the goods are not the consumers, and where the aim of the producers has been to provide the greatest quantity of goods at the lowest possible cost, for the greatest number of consumers. Growth has been the principal aim of almost all companies, on the basis that the larger a company, the more efficient it becomes, and the greater its profits.

As a result the consumer is offered increasingly standard products, such as Coca-Cola, Rothmans, cigarettes, Parker pens, Ford cars and so on. The suppliers are the multinational companies whose aim is to centralise their activities on a worldwide scale, in order to maximise their profits.

Yet today there are signs of revolt by the consumers against these standardised products. One example is beer, where pub drinkers have become disenchanted with national brews and demand individual, locally brewed ales.

Second, there is a corresponding increase in the demand for a greater variety of life-styles, with people doing things for themselves, instead of having them done for them. You can see this in the growth of the Do It Yourself market, where people decorate their own homes, make their own wine, bake their own bread and service their own cars.

The significance of this development is that more and more specialised products of all kinds are being demanded. This is where the small business has its greatest strength because, as will be shown later, it is in the best position to supply specialised products and personalised services.

The conditions are right

The European Community is expected by 1992 to have amended the Treaty of Rome by the Single European Act, resulting in the free movement of goods within the Community, as well as the free movement of capital, people and services. In addition the EFTA countries will also participate in the free trade thus created. Some 300 standards will be harmonised, and currencies brought more closely together through the European Monetary System (EMS).

Hence, almost no British company will be able to ignore doing business in Europe, and while you may speculate whether this is to be classified as domestic or export business, you will be dealing with people of different nationalities, speaking different languages and having different behavioural patterns, which is what export is all about.

The time to start is now, since 1992 is not that far off, and I suggest you read two booklets, published by the Community, 'Europe Without Frontiers' and 'Europe 1992'.

Spreading the risk

When a company is restricted to supplying the demand for its goods or services to one country it is subject to fluctuations in the prosperity of that country, but not all countries prosper or decline at the same time. Even as world trade is generally in difficulties, Singapore is booming while Nigeria is suffering, Europe prospers as the USA starts to decline.

It is prudent to spread the risk, so when a small business becomes involved with export markets, as well as its domestic market, it stands less chance of suffering when the domestic market is in trouble.

Greater competitiveness

There is always the danger of a small business becoming complacent when the domestic market absorbs all its production, yet it has been found from experience that once a company is exposed to what competitors are doing in other parts of the world, it finds new ways of doing business of which it may have been previously unaware.

A small engineering company sent one of its engineers to the Hanover Trade Fair. When he returned, he was full of ideas he had picked up from the competition, which he later adapted with great skill to his own company.

More profitability

Contrary to a widely held belief, export can often be more rewarding than domestic business in terms of profit, or what should more properly be termed contribution to revenue.

Certainly no company should expand into export unless it is determined that the venture will be profitable. This aspect will be examined in detail, but there is no doubt that export trade can be highly profitable provided the costing and pricing are right.

Job satisfaction

As I and many others know from personal experience, there is considerable job satisfaction to be gained from exporting and, to an increasing number of people, job satisfaction is just as desirable as more money. There is much pleasure to be gained from persuading a recalcitrant foreign buyer, who was determined never to buy British, to place his order with you. Exporting is more than just a job, and it might revitalise your company if you became involved with it. If you happen to be overseas, say on holiday, and you see your company product being sold or used locally, you feel a sense of pride.

A sense of duty

Not many people are prepared to export solely because it is in the national interest, yet increasingly any company, large or small, must show it is acting in a responsible manner to the community in which it operates, if it wishes to survive. Nothing could be more responsible than earning much needed foreign currency for your country, and as an added bonus you might win a Queen's Award for export, or receive some other honour.

The advantages of a small company

Most small businesses to whom I speak about export point to the greater resources in materials, manpower and finance of the larger companies, such as Beecham, Shell, ICI, IBM etc, and conclude that without such resources export is not for them.

While it may be easier to begin exporting with massive resources, it is more likely that the operation will be wasteful, because expenditure cannot easily be controlled to the same degree as in a company where every penny counts.

Your challenge as a small business is to achieve profitable results with limited resources, and the best way to do this is to concentrate on the advantages you possess over the larger companies.

The ability to take quick action

A major disadvantage of a large company is its inability to react quickly to changes in the overseas market place. When I worked on the overseas side of a multinational company, I remember having to obtain the approval of no fewer than 12 people before I could take any major decision. By then, more often than not, the opportunity I had wished to exploit had been lost.

A good example of a small business taking quick action to export is the Suffolk company which caters for thousands of people whose feet are never really comfortable in off-the-shelf shoes, or who are outside the normal range of sizes carried by retailers. They have a system whereby a retailer can take the foot measurements of people who want specially designed shoes, and then send the details to Suffolk, where the shoes will be made. They are not cheap, but people with odd feet are prepared to pay for the shoes to be specially produced, a task no large manufacturer of shoes seems willing or able to undertake. The small business calls this 'not getting too big for your boots'.

Exporting is easier

This may surprise you, but it is often easier to carry out an export transaction when a small number of people are involved. For instance, the processing of an export order is more easily monitored when only one person is doing it, and can say at once to which stage it has progressed.

Collecting a full set of documents called for against a documentary letter of credit will generally be accomplished more correctly the fewer people involved.

Moreover, mistakes can be more easily rectified when the responsibility for making them can be pinpointed to one person. In a large company it seems generally impossible to find out where the fault occurred, so it is more difficult to prevent the same thing happening again.

The personal touch

On my frequent travels around the world, I have found that the most common complaint from importers is that when buying from large exporters, they seldom get to know who actually deals with their business. 'Every letter I get bears a different signature,' is a frequent complaint.

In many smaller overseas countries, everyone knows everyone else, and that is how business gets done. Your great advantage as a small exporter will be that your customers, however far away they may be, will quickly get to know you, if only from correspondence. Hence, in many cases, they will prefer to deal with you.

Service

Your success will, to a major degree, be measured by the quality of the service you provide, and it seems that this is easier to accomplish in a small company.

In a sense, everyone is selling service, and it is the provision of a good and efficient service that should be the aim of every exporter. Yet another common complaint I meet overseas is that the service provided by exporters is bad, and this criticism is more often than not directed at the larger exporters.

It has always seemed crazy to me that after you have spent a great deal of time and effort getting a customer, you lose him because you give him poor service. It happens less often with Japanese, German or French exporters, so why should it occur with the British?

Financial resources

Do not be deterred by a lack of means to finance the exports. There is an extensive range of sources of finance available for the smaller business, details of which are clearly set out in *Raising Finance*, 3rd edition, by Clive Woodcock (Kogan Page, 1988). We shall examine some of the ways in which you can raise money to support your exports in Chapters 8 to 10.

Manpower resources

Many small companies shy away from export because they have no one in the company with the necessary experience to handle it. Let me suggest that this can be an advantage in itself, because instead of being saddled with separate domestic and export personnel, a small company can, from the outset, incorporate overseas business into its existing home trade.

Moreover, exporting is not all that difficult, in spite of what the experts will claim. Much of what you need to know will be found in this book. You can, in any case, buy in from outside any particular help you need on an *ad hoc* basis, help which will often be of greater value because it is from outside, and therefore more objective than when it comes from within the company.

Company loyalty

Exporting is essentially team-work, so a small company which can avoid endless committees, meetings and company 'politics' can more easily obtain that team-work, and engender a real sense of company loyalty into its operations.

I have often been appalled by the lack of loyalty shown to larger companies by their personnel. In my experience, working for a multinational company seems to consist of spending three-quarters of your time working for yourself, and only a quarter for the company, because of the incessant manoeuvring inherent in large companies.

It is perhaps significant that at present 'small is beautiful' seems to be the trend in companies, and that 'bigness is best' is on the way out, as large companies seek to hive off many of their subsidiaries, and hand over ever more responsibilities to their remaining divisions. This is why I maintain that there never has been a better time for a small business to start exporting.

To sum up the advantages of being a small company in export, take the example of British Island Airways. They pick up much profitable business from Air Florida's transatlantic flights by taking their passengers on to Brussels and Amsterdam. This flexibility enables a small airline to compete with the giants and flexibility is what a small company possesses in export which a large company does not.

Decisions you should take

Before you finally decide to enter the export field, however, there are certain decisions you should take in order to avoid the risks of failure.

Export seriously or not at all

Do not export if you have the idea that it will provide you with free holidays abroad at the company's expense, a cynical remark that has been made in many a board room.

Do not export for the look of the thing, which usually means the company is afraid that if it does not export, it may be penalised by the government in some way.

The danger is that if you export casually you will never take it seriously and this will always show. It has taken a long time for Britain's amateur approach to sport to be eradicated. Unfortunately it still remains to some degree in business, and often in export. You must decide to export in as highly professional a way as possible, which means taking it as a serious and lasting part of your business. There is no room for the amateur when you attempt to sell to customers overseas.

Do not merely export surplus production

A medium-sized company decided that the way to export was to take each week the total number of units it had manufactured and allocate them, first, to its domestic customers. The balance was then given to the export sales manager to sell overseas. Some weeks he had tens to sell, other weeks he had hundreds. He did his best until his customers refused to order on the basis that they never knew when they would get delivery. The domestic market collapsed, but by then there were no export customers left either. The company went into liquidation.

You cannot succeed in export if you merely try to export surplus production. You must decide from the outset that you will treat all customers, wherever they happen to be, on exactly the same basis as regards deliveries, from which it follows that you cannot start exporting unless you are sure you can maintain the additional production you hope to sell.

Do not use marginal costing or pricing

A favourite and potentially dangerous habit of many companies, when they start to export, is to cost and then price on a marginal basis. This means that, having absorbed all their fixed or overhead costs, they then add on a margin to cover their additional variable costs of materials and labour, thereby adding to their contribution to revenue. It is a tempting policy, but a bad one, because it is not making export revenue show a true contribution to the company. There are occasions when marginal costing and pricing are permissible, but it should seldom, if ever, be adopted as standard company policy.

Involve the whole company

I have already suggested that you should not decide export is impossible because you do not have the necessary staff to handle it. In fact, you should decide that from the beginning all your staff will be involved with export, and that you will not set up separate domestic and export divisions or departments. This will save you money and at the same time produce a better result, because there will be no conflict between the needs of customers at home or overseas — especially important for the European Community.

You will also avoid the mistake, so commonly made, of paying staff involved with export at a lower rate than those on the domestic side. Exporting must not be the poor relation in the company. It must involve everyone, from the shop floor up to the boss.

Objectives

By now you should have been able to make up your mind whether you feel exporting may be for your company. Assuming your answer is yes, your next task is to set yourself some objectives which, as you will know, must be realistic, measurable and achievable within your resources. Before doing so, however, take stock of what your company is already doing, and try to answer the following questions.

What business am I in?

It is no use saying, 'I am in the open-cast mining business'. What you really mean is that you are in the earth-moving business, so if open-cast mining declines, you can adapt your expertise to other aspects of moving earth. A small manufacturer of wooden wine casks watched the demand for the casks decline, and his business disappear, when he should have turned his attention to making something else out of wood, such as toys or furniture, since his expertise lay in handling wood.

It is the answer you give to this question which will define the parameters within which you can work, when you decide whether or not to take up the opportunities presented to you by customers overseas. You will seldom wish to extend beyond your existing skills, but as a small business you can easily adapt those skills to producing exactly what customers overseas want, provided you have a clear picture of the business you are in.

What is my particular expertise?
You must then decide whether your expertise lies in manufacturing, selling or innovating. A few of you will reply that it lies in all three. Yet many will recognise that they are better at one or the other, and if this is the case, then decide that your export objective should be to concentrate on that one.

The Japanese maintain that manufacturing is more effective if divorced from selling, and much of their worldwide success is attributable to their having companies which produce goods and separate companies which sell them, a system similar to that of the merchant adventurers of Elizabethan England.

Your objectives could be to manufacture for others to export the finished goods; to sell overseas what others make; to license companies overseas to make and sell your product; or, if you feel able to operate on a larger scale, to do all three.

Which countries do I know best?
With the world in front of you a difficult decision is to know where to start. Most people will have travelled overseas, if only on holiday. Most of you will know more about certain parts of the world than others, because you have studied or read about them, learned the language at school, or have seen these places on television.

Your objective, I suggest, should be to start at the place you know best, other things being equal. You might also add places which you like best, because you tend to do better the more you are in sympathy with your local surroundings.

Whom do I know best?
Another way of deciding where to start is to concentrate on those parts of the world where you know people, be they

17

relatives, friends or business acquaintances. It has always been true that it matters more whom you know than what you know, and this is certainly true of export. It is always a comforting thought that whatever you want to know, someone will have the answer.

So before you start trying to export, contact everyone you know around the world and see what they have to say. It will not cost you much and may produce some useful results.

The next steps

You will need to formulate some company objectives, both as regards handling business in the European Community and in countries outside the Community, even if the latter have to take second place to those covering Europe.

As time goes by you will need to be more precise about company objectives than you can be at present, but remember that it is no use saying, 'I want to sell as much as I can in Europe', or 'I want to sell all I can produce in other countries'. These are not objectives, but merely pious hopes.

When you have finished reading this book you will see that you must quantify your objectives in terms of what is to be exported, to whom and where, at what cost and for what contribution to the company's revenue. You will also learn how these quantified objectives can be met; that is, the strategies to be used.

You should also be able to answer the six questions I posed at the beginning of this chapter and decide whether export is for you, although with the advent of 1992 it seems that some export is inevitable for most small businesses.

Finally, remember to have a word with your accountant, and show him the sort of figures you have in mind and the facilities you will need. Price Waterhouse have an excellent small booklet called 'Exporting with Enthusiasm', while if you are thinking specifically of the Community they also have produced '1992 Guide for Small Businesses'.

Chapter 2

What Do I Need To Know?

The quick answer to this question is that you need to know the minimum necessary to prevent you making avoidable and costly mistakes.

Problems with export research

Most research produces no tangible results in the way of revenue, so as a small business, you cannot afford to spend a great deal of time and money on it. You cannot ignore it completely, however, or you may, as one large company did, send out Spanish sales literature to Brazil where they speak Portuguese. This was both a costly and an avoidable mistake.

Research into markets overseas will not guarantee success. It will produce facts about what is being bought, or why a certain product is popular. It will show you the economic conditions in any part of the world, but it falls down when it comes to forecasting what is likely to happen in the future. It will not say with certainty that if you do this, then that will follow. Presented with data you still have to take the decision as to what should be done.

Another problem with export research is that it applies to everything you do, so it is difficult to isolate it in a single chapter. Here we will consider what you need to know about the world market place in general, and where you can obtain this essential information as quickly and cheaply as possible. How research is carried out, and who, in a small business, should be responsible will also be covered. But research into what you are selling, to whom you wish to sell it, how you do this and how you get the goods or services to the customers, will be dealt with in each appropriate subsequent chapter.

A more serious problem is that there is too much information available, so your main task will be to decide what you need to know, and even more important, what is of little interest to you. All that information you can discard, concentrating only on what you must know to avoid mistakes. For example, if you sell baby foods, your interest is in mothers with small babies. Total population figures are, therefore, of academic interest, and can largely be ignored.

I suggest your attitude should be a cautious one, learning enough to prevent you making mistakes, and finding out where you may have gone wrong. Not until they had asked questions did a soap company, trying to sell washing powder to housewives in a certain African country, realise that you cannot use soap powder when your washing is done in the local river. They solved this problem, incidentally, by selling washing bowls along with the powder.

You must also recognise that research is all too often a good excuse for not taking any action, while much research is done primarily to prove that an opinion is correct. A small business must, therefore, learn to get along with the minimum amount of research, while recognising that there are certain things that should be found out before any action is taken.

The world market place

Before you start exporting you will need to have in your mind a brief outline of the world's market place, the conditions under which you have to operate, conditions over which you have no control. On the other hand, according to local conditions, you can alter what you sell and decide to whom you will sell it, so these are factors over which you *can* exercise control. World conditions can best be analysed under four headings.

Geographical conditions

Your knowledge of world geography should be as up to date as possible because, for example, countries and towns have a habit of changing their names. It is no use addressing your letters to Salisbury in Rhodesia, when you should have written to Harare in Zimbabwe.

A knowledge of the main sea ports is essential, as well as the position of the ports in relation to the towns they serve. If you wish to ship goods by sea to Kinshasa in Zaïre, they will go to the port of Matadi and face a long and difficult journey by rail or road up to Kinshasa, which necessitates your packing them extremely well if they are to arrive safely and undamaged. The advantage of shipping by air is that most airports are sited near the main towns, although if you despatch goods to Guyana, they will arrive at Timehri airport, which is a long and difficult 40 miles from Georgetown.

If your goods are affected by extremes of heat and cold, or wet and dry conditions, then climate will be an important factor. Climate can vary within a country — Nairobi is considerably cooler than Mombasa on the coast, which is invariably hot and sticky. Over an entire continent, climatic conditions vary even more, and you will need to know these variations if they affect what you sell.

Distances are another geographical factor which may affect your selling efforts. It is important to know, for example, that it is as far from New York to San Francisco as it is from London to New York, so it is no use expecting a representative on the east coast to deal with an after-sales problem on the west coast of the USA. Yet in a small, densely populated country such as Belgium, after-sales service can be handled by one company without a great deal of difficulty.

Mountains, rivers and deserts can be important factors since they influence where people live and the kind of lives they lead. In Egypt, for example, most of the people live around the river Nile, the lifeblood of that country. Mountains affect the performance of machinery, as anyone who has driven a car in the Andes will know. Desert people live a nomadic life, without settled homes.

You can, therefore, in many cases group countries overseas by their geographical conditions, where you should be looking for similarities rather than differences. If you sell air conditioning equipment, for example, you will be concerned to pick out those parts of the world where the climate is hot and sticky. If you sell anything that people eat, drink or wear you will need to group parts of the world according to their local geographical conditions, since they affect these products considerably. In India people prefer food which is hot and heavily spiced, and the same applies for Central America, where climatic conditions are similar.

If you decide to travel around the world as your exports increase, then you will need to know about geographical conditions for your journeys to be both pleasant and effective. You must know the best times to visit places, and equally important, the times to avoid. No one visits Australia in January when business people are mainly on holiday. You should not go to Johannesburg without warm clothes for the evening.

Political conditions

Since World War 2 it has been generally accepted that the world could be divided into two main political areas so far as trade is concerned. The first is the Communist bloc, or what is collectively known as COMECON (Council for Mutual Economic Assistance). This has handled virtually all international trade for the Communist countries, so if you wished to sell to them you could only deal with the various state buying agencies.

The second area is classified as the rest of the world, which includes both Communist and non-Communist countries. Here trade has been carried on in an infinite variety of ways, exporters being able to sell to both state and private sector organisations and individuals. The precise buyer is decided by the political conditions of the time. Malaysia, for example, tends to favour the private sector while Ghana has preferred the public sector.

Since the recent upheaval in the Eastern European countries this world political division is no longer valid. For example, exports to that area formerly known as East Germany have been radically affected by the recent unifications of East and West Germany. Trade with Germany is now likely to be channelled through the private rather than the public sector.

Hungary, Czechslovakia, Poland and Bulgaria are already receiving monetary aid from the rest of the world to enable them to buy essential equipment, some of which will probably be handled by the private sector. It is possible this could even apply within the USSR in the not too distant future.

Hence exporters must more than even concentrate on trying to anticipate political conditions in any countries where they wish to do business, and which are likely to affect imports. For example, will importing pass into the hands of non-whites in South Africa? Will Hong Kong remain the home of private enterprise after 1997? And what will be the position in the Middle East after the present upheaval there?

But while being enormously sensitive to political changes in the world an exporter should, of course, have no personal involvement with politics.

Economic conditions

Tariff and non-tariff barriers

From an economic point of view you may divide the world in three ways. First, trade is hampered by tariff and non-tariff barriers. Most countries impose tariffs on imports by means of customs duties. You must know, therefore, what customs duties your goods will attract overseas, since they will affect the local price.

In addition to tariff barriers, there is a whole series of non-tariff barriers to trade, the most common being a restriction on the amount of foreign currency an importer may have to pay for the goods he wishes to buy. Nigeria is using this method to limit her imports. Quotas for imports, which means that importers require a licence, is another way by which the purchase of goods from overseas is regulated. Mexico, for example, allows the import of essential items only and import licences are granted for these alone.

More subtle ways of limiting imports are the regulations imposed on goods which may be imported. It is mainly these unofficial regulations which are to be harmonised in the European Community by 1992. The USA, while preaching free trade, does its best to prevent it by imposing regulations on imports; for example, china must contain no lead. France insists that all documents connected with imports from other countries must be written in French. One of your first tasks as a new exporter will be to sort out the countries to which you can and cannot sell by reason of these unofficial barriers.

Natural resources

Second, the world may be divided by natural resources; that is, into the rich and poor countries or, if you prefer, the developed and developing nations. You can generally sell most goods, including quality consumer goods, to developed countries such as those in western Europe, North America, Japan, Australia and South Africa. It is between these countries that most trade takes place. You will, however, only be able to sell raw materials and the means of manufacturing other goods to developing countries in most cases. Hence, you can sell almost anything in a country like Switzerland, but will be able to sell virtually nothing in a country like Haiti.

Trading blocs

Because of the immense changes now taking place in Eastern European countries, it is likely that for the time being the only trading bloc of any note will be the European Community and the EFTA (European Free Trade Association) countries. Because of the close association between the Community and EFTA you can sell to virtually any country in western Europe with almost the same facility as you can sell in the United Kingdom.

The main difference between a free trade area and an economic community is that in the former the members make their own arrangements with other countries, whereas in the latter the arrangements are made by the community. And at present there is a small queue of countries, headed by Turkey, anxious to join the European Community.

Most small businesses would therefore be well advised to start by selling to other European countries. And while in due course this may become an extension of their domestic market, for the foreseeable future they will need to be treated as export markets because of their varying national characteristics. Moreover, each Eastern European country will have to be treated separately, on the basis of selling know-how (licensing); making barter arrangements; or entering into joint ventures.

Other free trade areas have not developed as much as has been envisaged, only ECOWAS (Economic Community of West Africa) showing any signs of activity.

Competition

There are two further economic conditions you will need to know. One is the imports of your particular kind of goods into a country, both from Britain and elsewhere, classified by both value and quantity. This information, with details of locally made equivalents, will give you some idea of the competition you will be facing.

Local currency

As we shall see, you will be paid in local currency, which will then be converted into sterling. You will probably also need to quote in the local currency of the market into which you are trying to sell. You therefore need to know about local currencies and their value in sterling.

Social conditions

This is the most interesting and possibly the most difficult information to get, because it affects your customers and their buying behaviour. Not all of it will apply in your case, so concentrate on those points relevant to your goods or services, and ignore the rest.

Language and the level of literacy apply to all export, because while you may manage with English to a large degree when dealing with customers overseas, sooner or later you will need to issue sales literature and instructions for use, or package your goods in the local language. The level of literacy will also indicate how far pictures instead of words have to be used. Of the 3000 or so languages in the world, happily you will need to become familiar with less than a dozen.

You may largely forget total population figures, and concentrate only on the number of people who are your potential customers. There may be over 100 million people in Indonesia, but less than 5 per cent will be buyers of imported goods.

Religious differences affect the sale of some products. For example, where the Moslem religion is predominant, as in the Middle East, liquor may not be sold, while in Saudi Arabia theatres, cinemas and drinking places are also prohibited.

At the same time religion may help you to sell. In the Republic of Ireland, for example, if the local parish priest approves of what you are selling then you are halfway to success.

Most people live in communities, known variously as classes or tribes, and these communities influence to a major degree what people purchase and how they behave. In Africa acceptance or rejection of a product by one tribe will often influence other tribes. The predominance of the Kikuyu in Kenya is a case in point.

Differences in race account for other buying habits. In Malaysia, for example, the power is shifting away from the Chinese in favour of the Malays, especially in government. So if you sell to government, then the Malays are now your target.

Money is often the measure of power and influence, and in most Latin American countries, where wealth is concentrated in a small percentage of the population, you will find that you only need to know a few families to have your goods accepted. In Ecuador, for example, power is in the hands of some 50 families.

Status is almost universal, whether it is conferred by money, family or education, so you should pick out those people with status, because what they buy will also be bought by others. Pop stars, famous footballers, television stars, movie actors and actresses all influence what ordinary people buy, because they set the fashion. Even with industrial goods, status is important because there is a kind of snobbery exercised by buyers. In many African countries a new gadget on a minister's desk almost certainly appears on everyone else's desk within a short time. In Turkey I saw an order for a computer go to IBM because the head of the company was convinced that all the best companies in the world used IBM computers.

One of your tasks in export will be to give your product some kind of status since it is one of the most powerful selling themes there is.

The family still plays a dominant part in any society, although it is often difficult to decide which member of the family is responsible for purchasing goods, as opposed to who pays for them. In the Middle East women generally play a subservient role to the men, who adopt a distinctly chauvinistic attitude to their women. In France there is a similar attitude, but in small businesses it is so often the women who hold the purse strings, and you find yourself selling to 'grand-mère'. In the United States, however, you may find 'junior' taking many of the family buying decisions, although there are signs of a revolt among American parents against the power exercised by their children.

In Japan the favourite saying of the men is something like, 'Keep your mouth shut and walk behind me'. Japanese men can have girl friends while their wives stay at home, yet I suspect that the Japanese men are nothing like so powerful as they would have you believe, and domestically may be extremely weak.

These social conditions will not affect all exporters to the same degree, but you should try to become familiar with those which may concern your products or services. If this mass of information sounds formidable, all you are doing is to learn what you already know about your own country. As a small company you have the advantage, moreover, of only needing to obtain it for a comparatively small number of countries, as opposed to the larger exporters who must acquire it for virtually the whole world.

Sources of information

For a start you will need a good atlas, one of the best being *The Times Atlas of the World*. *Lloyd's Loading List* — which you will need for details of shipping services — gives details of the world's sea ports. A British Airways timetable shows the names of the major airports, and their distances from the cities.

The essential information about countries can be obtained from the series of booklets called 'Hints to Exporters', issued by the Department of Trade and Industry. Another source of essential information are the country sheets issued with Croner's *Reference Book for Exporters*, which you will need for the details of documents required for shipping to any part of the world. Most of the banks supply helpful leaflets about trading conditions in major countries, such as Midland International's series of 'Spotlights'.

There are numerous other sources of information, such as the publications of the United Nations agencies, the Organisation for Economic Co-operation and Development (OECD), the European Community, the International Monetary Fund, the World Bank and so on. However, I suggest you only consult these if you need more detailed information than is available from the 'Hints to Exporters' series.

You can obtain details of British exports from the statistics compiled by HM Customs and Excise, and you can find these in the libraries of the Department of Trade and Industry, the London Chamber of Commerce and so on.

To keep up to date with the political, economic and social conditions of the world you will need to read a good deal. I suggest the *Financial Times*, *London Commerce* (published by the London Chamber of Commerce), and the *Economist*, which are essential, along with the *Export Times*, *Overseas Trade*, the export publication of the DTI, and *Export*, from the Institute of Export.

Export research

The first place to apply to is the Department of Trade and Industry, who have several export information services to offer the exporter. You should start by contacting your local regional office of the Department. (See page 165 for addresses.) The local office will be able to give a fair idea of your chances of success in the export field, obtaining the information from the Department's 16 market branches which between them cover virtually the whole world. These branches, moreover, can call on the services of the commercial staff of nearly 200 embassies and high commissions, providing information on anything from tariffs and regulations to local marketing methods, as well as the local economic and commercial climate.

You should also talk to your local regional office of the Department about its Marketing Initiative. This provides independent professional advice about export potential, how to plan for exporting, and how to select the right countries to attack. This scheme, run by the Institute of Marketing, offers from five to fifteen days of subsidised consultancy by an export specialist. The Department will pay half the cost, or two-thirds if the company is in an Assisted Area or Urban Programme Area.

If you wish to study statistics or other published information about countries overseas and their possibilities for you, you may do this in the DTI's Export Library in central London.

If you still need to carry out research before you start exporting, obtain from your regional office details of the Department's Export Marketing Research scheme. It offers free professional advice on how best to set about marketing research and help with half the cost, whether you commission your study from independent consultants or carry it out yourself.

There are several other services provided by the DTI but these will be dealt with in other chapters. Also note that there is a Small Firms Service, which aims to provide information free of charge on starting up a business, of which exporting is one example.

Almost as useful is the help now offered by the Association of British Chambers of Commerce, as you can see from their excellent booklet 'Export Services', which details the help a small business may obtain from its local Chamber of Commerce. This may well have an EDA (Export Development Adviser) whose job it is to help a new or small exporter to develop coherent and practical plans for export. The London Chamber of Commerce, for example, also runs numerous seminars and conferences on various aspects of export practice, in addition to organising numerous trade missions overseas, and has set up a small firms group to provide export intelligence from virtually all over the world.

The Institute of Export has an Export Specialists Service, using members to help companies to export, although this service has to be paid for. There is a new service offered by the British Exporters Association (BExA) (formerly the British Export Houses Association). This Association plans to promote the exports of the new and up-and-coming businesses which have developed from Britain's old industrial base, for the benefit of both its members and manufacturers in general. It also aims to bring together traders, the financial sector and manufacturers in developing export trade.

Other organisations which will help the new or small exporter are the Confederation of British Industry, the British Institute of Management, the Institute of Marketing and the British International Freight Association. You should contact these if you are in need of specialist advice.

Test marketing

While some research is undoubtedly necessary for a new exporter or a small exporter expanding his business, the aim should, I suggest, be to keep research to a minimum because it costs money and no revenue accrues from it. Moreover, it does not necessarily help the small business to decide what to do because it so often produces an unhelpful answer.

One way round this problem is to test market; that is, to try to sell in one or more parts of the world and use the experience gained to show you what you are doing correctly or where you are going wrong. To make test marketing really effective you should choose areas and schemes which are comparable as far as possible, in order to be able to determine which produces the best results. For example, you might try selling in Belgium or Switzerland to give yourself some indication of how you would fare in the rest of Europe. Or if you are anxious to consider North America as a market, start by tackling the area in Canada south of Toronto, around Windsor, and then expand south across the border into the USA around Chicago. If you can sell there, you can probably sell anywhere in North America.

Test marketing as a research technique is rather more complicated than I have suggested but for a small business it often provides a quick and cheap way of finding out what is possible.

Other DTI services

While as a small business you will not be concerned with the DTI's large-scale projects service, since this is normally involved with projects worth over £20 million, you may like to know that the Department's Export Intelligence, to which you must subscribe, sends out details of specific export opportunities. You say in which areas you are interested and you will receive details of opportunities within three days of their arrival in the Department.

The other service, which is called Trade Through Aid, covers the opportunities to supply goods purchased by multilateral development agencies such as the World Bank, various agencies of the United Nations etc. Not all such purchases are large so some may be of interest to you even as a small business.

Trade missions

Clearly the best way to carry out research into prospects in overseas countries is to visit them, but for a small company this can prove to be an expensive form of research. One way out of this problem is to go on what the DTI calls an outward mission.

These missions can be organised by a trade association, a Chamber of Commerce or any approved non-profit making body. Most are run by Chambers of Commerce and trade associations, as well as by such bodies as the Institute of Export.

Normally between ten and twenty people go on a mission, which may visit a single country or a group of countries, but remember, this scheme does not apply to countries in western Europe, North America or around the Mediterranean. The great advantage for a small business is that, instead of visiting a country with little prior knowledge of what to do or whom to see, the trade mission is organised by people who know what contacts should be made and how to arrange them. On completion of the mission the DTI will refund a proportion of the costs to each company representative, there being a scale of contributions for each country which has already been agreed. For example, a visit to Singapore entitles you to a contribution of about £700, and to Sri Lanka about £500, while to Australia and New Zealand it would be about £820.

On these missions you have the opportunity of carrying out your own research, of trying to sell, and in particular, of meeting the people locally you might otherwise never get to know. Having done your homework, you will probably find there is no better way for a small company to continue than by going on a trade mission. The London Chamber of Commerce runs about 60 a year, so there is no lack of opportunities.

European Community information

A new source of information specially designed for the small business has recently been set up in the Commission of the European Communities. This is a set of some 40 centres for

European business information, of which four are currently located in Britain. They are in London, Birmingham, Newcastle and Glasgow; see page 167 for addresses.

The objective of the centres is to provide businesses with up to 500 employees with information about the European Community, including market intelligence, public contracts, research and development programmes, finance and training, the idea being to integrate Community information with national requirements. Each centre works closely with the Community's main information centres in London and Scotland, and also with the Small Business Task Force in Brussels.

More centres are planned, since the Community is determined that the small business is given as much help as possible to survive in the new 1992 Community.

The collection of information

A small business should not, I suggest, rush out and hire an export research executive, or try to set up an export research department, certainly not in the initial stages.

To start, the company should make each section responsible for its own research. The sales people could collect information on customers; the transport side could cover transport conditions, the accounts people currencies and payment problems, and so on. This reinforces what I have already suggested, namely that export in a small business should be a team effort.

In order to co-ordinate and prevent duplication of effort there should be some central point where the information is kept, and a copy of the information should be held there. This can be under the care of a competent secretary, who could also ensure that the information is seen by all who need it. This central store of information can consist of files for each country, plus files for each activity, and should be started with all the information the company possesses, since even in a small company some information will already exist in the form of correspondence etc.

In this way, you can keep time and expenditure to a minimum, and this should be your attitude to export research. Should you need more help you can hire a consultant on an *ad hoc* basis; a retired export manager or a redundant one, might be the answer.

Another way of obtaining information would be to approach your local technical college or polytechnic, and offer their

31

export students a chance of carrying out some research as part of their studies. The Business Studies Department would probably be only too willing for this kind of work to be done by the students; certainly at Central London College we are always willing to allow students to do some research for companies in the London area as part of their work, and most colleges will do the same.

As I said earlier, research involves every aspect of exporting, so you will also have to research what you are hoping to export and the prices at which you hope to sell it. You must find out why your potential customers might or might not buy, and look into means of transport and methods of payment and insurance.

There will always be information you feel you would like, but keep this side of exporting research to a minimum, and remember that before you decide to obtain information you must know what you are going to do with it when it comes, since there is no point in obtaining information unless it can be put to good use.

Chapter 3
What Can I Export?

The quick and reassuring answer to this question is that you can export almost anything you sell at home in some form or another; few companies can claim that what they produce is unexportable. You should, however, already have decided what business you are in, and analysed the particular skills your company possesses. These will indicate the parameters of what you are likely to wish to export. You should also have decided if you wish to make and sell, to sell only, or to export no more than your skills. Assuming that you wish to manufacture and sell goods of some kind, or to sell what another manufacturer makes, what properties should an export product possess?

The ideal export product

There is, of course, no such thing as an ideal export product, but you should try to ensure that it fulfils as many of the following conditions as possible.

You can make enough of it

I put this first because so many small companies have started to export with great enthusiasm but insufficient production capacity, and then regretted they ever tried exporting. You must ensure that your raw materials are available, and your labour and machinery are equal to the extra demands export is going to make. It is of little use being unable to meet a demand, because this merely antagonises the buyers who turn to something else. This is a particularly important point when considering to which country you will export. Selling to the USA, for example, is often beyond the productive capacity of small businesses, unless they are able to limit sales to a section of the American market.

You can make it to the specifications required

As a small business you will have the advantage over a larger company because you should more easily be able to adapt to varying specifications. If you sell beds, for example, you will find the beds in Germany tend to be larger than in Britain, and similar considerations apply to clothing and footwear. In Jamaica, for instance, men tend to want trousers with larger 'behinds' than elsewhere, because that is the way men are built, so slimline is unsuitable. Dutch women tend to have larger feet than those in France. So you will need to be flexible in meeting precise specifications overseas.

It has the edge on the competition
There must be something about an export product which gives it an edge over the competition. If you export industrial jigs and tools, you must be able to claim that they are more durable, or made to greater degrees of tolerance, than the others, otherwise there is no reason why customers should buy them.

It is simple to use
There is often a tendency for manufacturers to make products so complicated that, unless the user is in a high technology field, he is unable to find sufficiently skilled labour to use them. This is particularly important when you export to developing countries. A hand drill, for instance, must be simple to operate and foolproof in use, with no complicated assembly instructions.

It needs little or no service
You will have noticed the trend towards products which require virtually no service, because service is always difficult to provide in another country. An ideal export product should need no service, like the modern car battery which does not have to be topped up every few days. Many people in less developed countries do not understand a need for service, and merely complain when something wears out because of not being properly maintained. The disposable cigarette lighter was produced to save service, and you should try to avoid the necessity for service wherever possible.

It suits local conditions
We saw in the previous chapter that conditions vary considerably throughout the world, especially as regards temperature, humidity and so on. Ideally, any export product should be capable of standing up to all these conditions. If you export clothing, weights of cloth must be suited to the climate and

synthetic materials avoided. A battery torch is no use if it is adversely affected by damp.

It conforms with the local laws
Legal restrictions on what may or may not be sold are proliferating worldwide, and nowhere perhaps as fast as in the EC. This is particularly so in the case of foodstuffs, toiletries, medicines and chemicals. Even textiles must be labelled with details of the fibres from which the materials are made, together with the percentages of contents, such as cotton 85 per cent and polyester 15 per cent. This is not only to show what the customer is buying but also to help in washing and cleaning.

Its process has been patented
If you wish to export a product which is the result of a special process, you must ensure that the process is patented in every country where it is likely to be sold. For this you will need the services of a patent agent, which you can obtain by applying to the Institute of Patent Agents. There is also a European Patent Office in Munich, where you can register patents which will be protected in all EC countries and some European countries outside the Community. Your patents will not, however, always be respected in Communist countries.

The product is needed
One way of finding out if there is a need for a product is to ask your customers to let you know what requirements they have. A small business which supplied electric measuring equipment was told that there was a need for electronic measuring devices. So they set about designing oscilloscopes and vacuum type bridges, knowing that there was an existing market. Encourage your customers to ask you first if they have needs, in case you can supply them.

Few products meet all these requirements, but to export successfully your product should meet at least some of them. Moreover, it will be your ability to respond quickly to changing market conditions which will ensure success. Far too many companies, especially those in the industrial field, insist on trying to sell what they make, instead of making what they have found they can sell. If you buy to resell you must persuade your suppliers to produce what you know you can sell, and not accept what they wish to supply, if you feel it is not entirely suitable. This is one of the reasons for the Japanese success in the export world, which we in Britain would do well to copy.

Product modifications

An ideal export product would need no modifications since it would be saleable anywhere in the world without alterations. Few such products exist, although if you export worms for bait, as one Essex company does, you do not have to alter the worms. Nor do you have to change daffodils if you send them overseas.

~ Most manufactured products will require some modifications, although your aim should be to keep these to a minimum. Moreover, when searching for customers, as we shall see in Chapter 5, your objective will be to find people who want and will buy something which is as nearly identical as possible to that sold elsewhere in the world. The kinds of modification you may have to consider are as follows:

The materials used

If you manufacture furniture, in France you will find a preference for mahogany, whereas in Germany they prefer oak. If you make cooking utensils, you may have to vary the materials according to the source of heat over which they are used. Neither of these changes should cause a small company any great difficulties, but if you find that changing the raw materials is too great a step for you, then you must dispense with those countries you cannot supply with your existing materials.

Technical specifications

There is an increasing worldwide tendency for these to become more demanding and varied, country by country. You can, however, obtain all the help you need from the Technical Help for Exporters (THE) section of the British Standards Institution, telephone 0908 221166. They publish a book *Technical Barriers* worth the £3 it costs, since it gives details of how countries control the design, manufacture, certification and use of individual products, as well as a useful check list of the points you need to bear in mind.

THE will also answer individual queries from companies on the regulations in force for a particular product in any overseas country, and provide details of the regulations, codes of practice and technical requirements needed to be able to sell them. For this service you have to pay, but the cost is minimal compared with the problems you would have without their experience and expertise. No small business should attempt to export without checking first with THE on the specifications required for a product in any particular country.

Size

We have already seen that a company selling clothing or footwear may have to contend with varying sizes in order to meet the needs of people in different countries. If you can be flexible about size, you may well pick up extra business, as a small soap company did when it produced toilet soaps in numerous sizes, such as special guest sizes, large bath sizes, and even family sizes. The giants of the soap business did not find it worth their while to do this, so the small company obtained the business.

Design

An example of design needing to be varied is that of tea or coffee services. In Britain we are accustomed to a milk jug being included in the set because we tend to drink tea and coffee with milk. Yet in many parts of Europe and elsewhere tea and coffee are drunk black, so there is no need for a milk jug. The Design Centre in London is a mine of useful information on design requirements all over the world.

Colour

Many countries have distinct preferences when it comes to colour, and the Design Centre will also help you here. The sort of problem you meet is that customers want a different colour from the one you are using. I remember trying to sell spades in Burma, where instead of red blades the customer insisted on blue. A large exporter held it was not worth his while making the change so the business went to a small company who were perfectly happy to supply the spades with blue blades.

In tropical countries pastel shades tend to lose their colour, so it is advisable to use stronger colours than in Britain. Moreover, people tend to prefer bright colours to sober black. Radios, for example, are preferred in African countries with brightly coloured panels, because there is status in owning a radio, and more status in owning a brightly coloured radio, rather than a grey or black one.

Even machinery is often preferred if it is brightly coloured. When selling to developing countries, it is easier to issue

37

instructions for use if you can refer to different coloured parts, instead of having to describe them. Avoid subtle shades which may not be understood.

Your aim must be to strike a reasonable balance between standardisation and the modifications required, even if this means limiting the number of places to which you can export. You must ensure that the modifications are allowed for in your costs, but as a small company, you should be able to make them more cheaply and easily than a large firm.

You will appreciate that to achieve this calls for the closest co-operation between sales and production. If you are an engineer-dominated company, you must not allow production to determine what you make for export, but insist on the closest partnership between those who produce the products and those who sell them. You must aim to supply exactly what customers want, rather than what the engineers would like to sell them. This will also help you to formulate a clear policy regarding the modifications you will be asked to make by customers overseas.

There is help available for small companies on manufacturing problems from the Manufacturing Advisory Service (MAS), operated on behalf of the Production Engineering Research Association (PERA). There are also five Department of Trade and Industry Research and Development Boards, covering Textiles, Electronics, Chemicals and Materials, Mechanical and Electrical Engineering and Meteorology. Further help is available from the Rural Development Commission.

Product presentation

As a small business you will have to pay special attention to the presentation of your product, because you are competing with companies who can afford to promote themselves and what they sell on a much larger scale than you. The better your presentation the greater the impact you will have.

Packaging

If you produce goods which have to be packaged, you will probably find that you need to modify the packages in much the same way as you may have had to alter the product itself; you will need to consider the materials used for packaging: the size, colour, design and special requirements due to local legislation.

If, for instance, you sell any kind of foodstuffs where the calorie content is important, when you sell in Europe you will need to quote in kilojoules and not in calories. If you sell electrical goods, all countries have strict laws about the technical details which must be shown on the packages, together with information on how to use the appliances, how the plugs must be fitted and so on. Even with cosmetics, the ingredients must be detailed, together with the date by which the product must be used.

Colour is important on packages because of colours such as black and white being generally disliked overseas, whereas red and gold are usually favoured, and in Africa, green is a favourite colour.

The wording and illustrations have to be carefully considered, to ensure they are suitable for the local conditions. In multilingual markets such as Canada or Belgium you will need multilingual packages — in French and English for Canada, and French and Flemish for Belgium. Leaflets included in a package will have to be similarly treated.

The size and composition of packages may vary where, for example, the product is sold in single units, because the package must be capable of being opened and re-sealed easily and without damage.

Remember that in developing countries packages have a resale value and that products are often purchased because their packaging has a value in itself. I remember in Turkey being able to sell glass jars which had contained Nescafé, because their screw lids kept the contents airtight. In Lagos there is a second-hand package market, where packages are bought and sold.

Your aim should be to keep package variations to a minimum, consistent with the local regulations, because having different packages adds to the cost of production. When modifying a package costs too much for the business you are likely to obtain, you may have to give up selling.

You can obtain the help you will need with your packaging problems from THE, the Design Centre and the Research Association of the Paper and Board, Printing and Packaging Institution (PIRA).

Your company name
However small your company, you must present yourself to your customers overseas with a distinctive and easily

remembered company name. It should be set in a modern and attractive style, and if possible should reflect the kind of business you do. Remember that you will be competing against much larger exporters, who will have spent a great deal of money making sure their names are remembered, so your name has to work that much harder, because you will not be able to spend money publicising it.

If you sell industrial products you should ensure that your company name appears on them in some form, so that your customers are in no doubt who has made and supplied them.

Take a good look at your company name and the way it is used on your letterheads and other stationery. Try to imagine the effect of it on people many thousands of miles away who have probably never heard of you. And do not hesitate to change or improve it if necessary.

Brand names and trade marks
If possible your product should have either a distinctive brand name or trade mark, because in many parts of the world purchases are made on a mark, since this is often the only guarantee a customer has that it is the genuine article and not an imitation.

Admittedly, most well known symbols have already been used and registered, such as animals or flowers. But you can use numbers, or made up words, which have the advantage that they have no meaning in other languages, a trap that many exporters tend to fall into even today.

Both trade marks and brand names should be registered to prevent others using them, and the Institute of Trade Mark Agents will advise you how to go about doing this overseas.

Finally, remember that because everyone in the world today continually wants something new, you should continually be updating both your product and the way it is presented. So why not start by putting one star or crown on it now, and then bring out a two-star or two-crown model, and so on. It is amazing how customers like to feel they have the very latest version, and will buy a new one if only to impress their friends and neighbours.

Selling know-how

So far we have only considered a small business making and exporting a product, but for many smaller companies, producing greater quantities may not be an activity in which they wish to engage. Moreover, in view of the increasing number of tariff and non-tariff barriers to international trade, many countries are unable, or reluctant, to import from Britain. In these cases, the company has the option of having goods manufactured in the country concerned, and also of allowing the manufacturer to sell them locally. So what the original small company sells are skills, not products.

The basis of licensing

You should initially already have patented your manufacturing process and registered your brand name and trade marks. These form the basis of what you have to sell, or what in legal terms is called your 'property'. You then sell the right to a company in another country to make and/or sell your product under licence from yourselves.

For many companies, this is one of the best ways to export because you are earning foreign currency for comparatively little effort, and using only your existing resources. For this reason, it is an ideal answer to many small businesses who ask, 'What can I export?'

The value put on your property will depend on the value of the process you have to sell, along with the value of your name and trade mark. Clearly a licence to make and sell Kodak cameras would be more valuable than one to make and sell an unknown camera. But any small business with a patented, highly technical process has something saleable.

This sale of know-how will not only enable you to sell behind high tariff barriers, it will also enable you to sell in countries where sales are difficult because of intense competition (such as Western Germany or Japan) and where you may not wish to become directly involved.

Remember that by licensing others in this way you will forfeit your right to do business there yourself, so do not rush into licensing lightly. You cannot easily withdraw a licence, and no one will buy one valid only for a short time.

Procedure for licensing

You must first let it be known that you have some property to sell in a particular country, usually by advertising.

You must advise any would-be purchaser what exactly you are selling. It may be the right to manufacture; or the right to make and sell; or the right to manufacture with some or all of

41

the raw materials supplied by yourselves. If you can arrange the latter, then you will gain by selling the materials as well as the licence.

You then specify what information you will supply, and what you expect your licensee to contribute, because licensing is a two-way business, and there is no reason why you should not benefit from any expertise developed by your licensee when making your product.

Next, arrange for some form of quality control over what is produced under licence, because you must not allow your reputation and that of your product to suffer from poor quality. This is not always easy to arrange or monitor, but it must be done by some means of inspection at regular intervals.

As to price, licences are usually sold first for an initial cash sum; additionally, there should be an annual royalty on all sales made. You will be wise to insist on a minimum annual royalty, whether sales have been made or not, to ensure that your licence is not bought with the intention of keeping your product off the market. If you are supplying some or all of the raw materials, then you must agree your selling price of these, on which you will hope to make an additional profit.

All this will need to be put into a formal agreement which will follow closely the kind of agency agreement mentioned in Chapter 5. To make sure you receive your royalties you will need to insure their receipt, as explained in Chapter 10.

Although this may sound like a fairly simple operation, there are several professional skills involved, and you should obtain all the help you can from the Licensing Executives Society, which has branches in some 19 countries.

Licensing is most suitable for companies which spend a good deal on research and development, and for those which are more interested and expert in producing new things rather than trying to sell them. Instead of trying to break into the European markets, a small company which makes specialised paints used in building ships of all shapes and sizes has licensed the production of these paints in each country because paint is a difficult product to export. It thus receives a very reasonable return for virtually doing no more than supply expertise to its licensees.

Licensing can also be applied to services, such as we have seen in Europe with the franchising of Wimpy Bars. There seem to be endless opportunities in education, where colleges can license the use of their names and some of their facilities in other countries. In fact, any service with a well known name, and some expertise, can be licensed for use in other countries.

It cannot be stressed too strongly that for many small businesses licensing is a way of exporting which should always be explored. It overcomes the problems of increased production which are bound to arise, while few small companies will be able to invest money in joint ventures to manufacture overseas. So take a good look at your own property, and see if it is saleable for exploitation overseas.

Opportunities for the export of goods

It would be virtually impossible to list all the export opportunities for goods from small companies, but a few examples may suggest ideas which you might be able to take up.

As I have already said, the Do It Yourself market is expanding all over the world, and anything which will help people to do work for themselves seems assured of a good future; for example, the provision of special kits, or packages of flour or yeast, with which to bake bread; the provision of new wall coverings and paints for home decorating and repairs; the provision of self-servicing kits for motor cars and trucks.

The leisure market is also expanding, as people tend to have more leisure and seek something to fill this free time. Apart from sports gear, toys and games, especially in the video field, have you noticed the growth of executive toys for people in offices? Then there are the embroidery kits, the furniture which can be assembled in the home, the painting sets and the home computers.

In the food market, what people overseas wish to buy from Britain are the speciality foods. In Belgium, for example, I was amazed to find few cheeses from Britain, and the same applies in other European countries. Locally made spiced sausages, pâtés, and even black puddings would seem to have possibilities. There is a good example of biscuits quoted in *Raising Finance* by Clive Woodcock. A small firm I know does a nice line in exporting cakes.

While Britain exports daffodils, there seem to be few exports of indoor plants, yet all over the world there is a strong fashion for these in people's homes.

There is a growing market for second-hand machinery. One company which distributes tractors in Britain does a brisk trade with Sweden in the tractors it takes in part exchange for new ones.

43

Reproduction furniture, built by craftsmen, is a growing industry, and the same approach can be used in the cutlery and jewellery fields, because of the demand for anything but mass produced articles.

Crime has become such big business worldwide that there are now increasing opportunities for crime prevention products, both for the home and for personal use.

Carriage clocks are back in favour again, and one small business is offering these engraved with the name of the recipient, a good example of a personalised product. Another is handmade sweaters, embroidered initials or names being added free of charge.

The high technology field is so important that the Department of Trade and Industry has set up a Small Engineering Scheme to help smaller companies to increase the competitiveness of their machine tools, welding machinery and metal working devices, all of which have good export prospects.

These are merely a few of the export opportunities which seem to exist, and they are mentioned in the hope that they may suggest opportunities for your own small company. Your principle should be to make willingly exactly what customers demand, and at all times to be flexible enough to adapt to local requirements.

It has been assumed that what you produce can be freely exported. As you will see in Chapter 7 there are certain goods for which an export licence is required. You should, therefore, enquire at the Export Licensing Branch of the Department of Trade and Industry to make sure your goods are not on the list of goods which either may not be exported, or may only be exported with a licence.

The export of services

If you study the British export figures over the past few years you will notice that the fastest growing area is that of services. There are many opportunities to export services, the most obvious being in the computer software field. The Department of Trade and Industry has a Software Products Scheme (SPS), which will give financial help to companies anxious to develop software business.

Most professional people, such as accountants, architects, quantity surveyors, engineers of all kinds, and designers, should be able to obtain business, especially from developing countries.

For example, there is a need for help with inflation accounting systems in many countries, while the amount of new building must require the services of engineers, quantity surveyors, designers and architects. In developing countries there is a never ending need for experts in drainage, sewage and water supplies. Another related field is waste disposal as the world produces more and more garbage, and getting rid of it is becoming an increasingly difficult problem.

Education and training, technical training in particular, are still greatly in demand. A small firm of insurance brokers regularly runs seminars overseas, as does a firm of shipping brokers.

Leisure services have a good future, along with goods for leisure activities. One example has been the success of dance halls and dancing classes in the United Kingdom, and experts in dancing and keep fit activities could extend their work abroad.

For help on exporting services, consult the British Invisible Exports Council.

Quality and service

If you examine complaints about British goods from importers in other countries, you will find that they are nearly always based on quality and service.

As a small business, you will be in the best position to ensure that whatever you offer to customers overseas is of the highest quality. You are unlikely to wish to export great quantities of anything, leaving that to the companies who specialise in fast moving consumer goods, produced in bulk. By concentrating on small quantities, small businesses can put quality first, and quality is what the world expects from Britain. It is not too late to restore that reputation. Moreover, quality goods, as we shall see in the next chapter, should return a higher contribution to the company's revenue than mass produced ones.

As regards service, customers demand not only service with their enquiries and orders, but also service for the goods they buy, in the form of an adequate supply of spare parts, replacement parts supplied free of charge if the original goods are faulty, and guarantees of performance. Where necessary an exporter should arrange locally available service facilities prior to supplying the goods, or be able to provide that service from Britain. Not all goods can be made disposable, and thus not require service. When an order is taken, spare parts should be included as part of the deal.

If you concentrate on quality and service, then your innovative and entrepreneurial skills should enable you to export almost any kind of goods or services to some part of the world.

Chapter 4
At What Price Can I Export?

Of all the decisions a small business will have to take, fixing the price at which the goods will be sold to customers overseas is probably the most crucial and often the most difficult. Your aim should be to obtain as high a contribution to your company's revenue from your exports as possible. How then can you price your goods to achieve this objective?

Revenue

Before you can decide how to maximise your contribution to revenue, you must first decide how you propose to calculate your revenue from exports. It is widely believed that revenue is the quantity of goods sold, multiplied by their price. If you sold 100 hammers at £5 each your revenue would be £500. This is partly true, but your accountant would say that revenue is the cash when you receive it, so that £500 would not be revenue until the customer had paid you. If the hammers were sold to a customer in Fiji, for example, you might well not be paid for a considerable time after you had sold them, bearing in mind the time it would take the hammers to reach their destination.

To the exporter, revenue should mean the financial results of sales made to export customers and should be calculated in the same way for each export sale, so you may compare the results of selling to customers in different parts of the world.

As you know, there are three main methods of calculating revenue. There is *total revenue*, which is the full amount received for the goods you have exported, or the full amount you expect to receive at a later date. Total revenue is important when you look at cash flow problems, the amount of working capital you need, and the cost of giving your customers the credit they will almost certainly demand. Second, there is *ex works revenue*, which is the total revenue from which has been deducted all money paid to people outside the company.

Third, there is *retained revenue*, which is what you have left from ex works revenue after paying for materials and so on which you have bought from outside suppliers. While ex works revenue can be used for comparison purposes, retained revenue is the added value, or return to the company for its own activity, and shows what a company gets for what it spends. Hence, it has to cover all fixed and variable costs, and whatever margin of 'profit', or contribution, is made to the company's revenue. As you will see, when we discuss costs, you must also include specific fixed costs when calculating your retained revenue, which should then be the basis on which to start your price calculations.

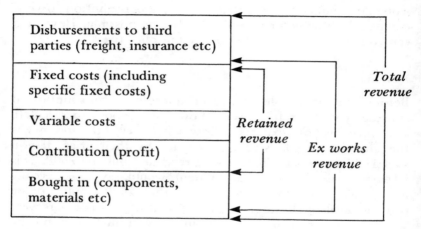

Costs

In economic terms, the cost of buying or selling anything is the cost of whatever else you might have done with the money, or the opportunity cost. It is a cost you never know, but in export you should continually evaluate the probable results of each option you have, so that you may arrive at the correct decision as to what is best for the company. For example, if you sell goods to a customer in Italy for £5000 when for the same expenses you could have sold them to a customer in Australia for £6000, while the accountant might tell us that for Italy we made a profit of £500, what he could not tell us is that we might have made a profit of £1500 had we sold to Australia.

We shall return to this aspect of costs later in the chapter, but for the moment we need to be more precise about costs. As you know, there are two basic kinds of costs, *fixed costs* which do not vary in relation to the quantity of goods produced, and *variable costs* which do vary, more or less, in relation to the quantity of goods produced. In essence, your fixed costs are your overheads incurred whether you produce anything or not. Your variable costs are the materials you use and the labour required to turn the materials into goods.

There is thus no such thing as a 'unit cost' of producing anything, because costs depend, first, on quantity. The cost of making one Concorde bears no relation to the cost of making 50. If you draw a graph showing your fixed and variable costs, plotted against the quantity produced, and then add in the revenue you would receive from selling the goods at a fixed price, you can see your break-even point, and the point at which you start to make some 'profit'.

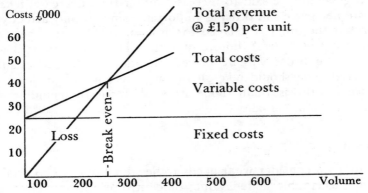

Figure 4.1 *Fixed and variable costs*

In practice, of course, fixed costs are not all that fixed, and should be divided into *general fixed costs*, which are incurred whether or not any sales are made, and *specific fixed costs* which are costs of selling and promoting the goods in a particular market. The former must be allocated over all exports, while the latter can be allocated to specific countries, and deducted from the retained revenue.

These specific fixed costs are what might be called semi-variable, in that they do not have to be incurred, and will cover the cost of research, visits overseas, selling costs in the form of commissions to third parties, and all forms of promotion. We looked at research in the previous chapter and the costs involved must, therefore, be allocated either to specific markets overseas or, if this is not possible, to general fixed costs.

The variable costs will apply differently to different companies, because labour, for example, may not be laid off in some companies if production falls, because of the difficulty of taking it on again if production is increased. In effect, you have perfectly variable costs and what might be termed semi-variable costs, and you should try to obtain accurate figures for both.

Hence, from retained revenue it is necessary to take away specific fixed costs, a proportion of general fixed costs and the known variable costs, and the residue will be the contribution made to the company's revenue.

There is one further factor regarding the variable costs of labour and materials. Since these change from time to time, and can generally be said to increase, rather than decrease, *when* a customer places an order is important, since it may affect your costs if the order is delayed for any length of time. Therefore, you may well insist, before quoting a price, on linking it with when the order will be placed, in addition to the quantity ordered. You should take all this into account when quoting a price and this is usually done, as we shall see, by including it in your conditions of sale.

Credit

Before we consider what needs to be added to costs to produce some acceptable added value, or contribution to revenue, and thus arrive at a basic cost on which to base your price, you must take into account the cost of credit, because in most cases, with orders from customers overseas, you will be out of your money for some considerable time.

You may take the cost of credit in two stages, the first being the length of time you will be out of your money up to the time the goods are shipped, and the second from then until the customer pays you.

To calculate the cost of these credits you take the rate at which you could borrow money. For most small companies this will be at least 4 to 5 per cent above the base lending rate of the banks. At present this is 10 per cent so it is fair to assume an average borrowing rate for a small company of 15 per cent, since it is unlikely it will be much, if at all, less, although it will vary according to the credit-worthiness of the company.

Assuming that it costs 15 per cent to borrow money and

supposing it takes you three months to despatch an order, which for purposes of credit will be 90 days, as all credit is calculated in units of 30 days, the cost of this will thus be:

$$\frac{90 \times 15}{365} = 3.70\%, \text{ or say } 4\%$$

that is, you multiply the number of days by the cost of the money and divide by the days in one year.

Then suppose the amount you wish to receive for the goods is £1500. Using a well known mathematical formula, turn the 4 per cent into a fraction, namely 1/25, and deduct one from the lower number, which makes 1/24. This part of your total of £1500 is £62.50, and is the amount you need to add to ensure that, if you are paid when the goods are despatched, you receive the full £1500 you intended.

Before you use this as a basis for your quotation, however, you must find out when your customer intends to pay you, because he may well ask for credit after the date on which the goods have been despatched. Suppose he asks for 90 days, then you must quote him the addition of 1/24 of £1562.50 to the total, which is £65.10 plus £1562.50, or £1627.60. You may then suggest a cash discount of £65.10, which would bring you back to the £1562.50 you required.

Of course the customer is paying for the credit, but then a customer ultimately pays for everything, and in this way you can agree to demands for credit without losing money yourself. So in addition to finding out how much a customer wishes to buy, and when he is likely to order, you must also find out when he intends to pay, all three factors affecting the price you quote him.

Contribution to revenue

Your next problem, when fixing a price, will be to decide what added value or contribution you wish to make to your costs, which will then only leave you to add the specific fixed cost of selling and promoting your goods overseas. Therefore, you should think in terms of a contribution which will allow adequate resources for your selling efforts, as well as leaving a reasonable residue for the company.

Except for one-off goods, to some degree you must decide whether you wish, for example, to sell 500 units with an added value of £10 each, making a contribution of £5000, or to sell

100 units with an added value of £50 each, which would give you the same total contribution. So contribution will depend partly on quantity, and partly on the competition, because their prices may well affect the price at which you can sell, and therefore the contribution you can expect to make.

Many companies adopt a policy of cost plus, that is to say they add a certain percentage to their costs, or a sliding scale of percentages according to the quantities produced. Generally, companies have a minimum and maximum percentage mark up, showing the greatest contribution they hope to make, and the lowest price below which they will not sell.

You can, of course, approach the problem another way, such as determining the total contribution you expect from exports, and leaving individual prices to achieve this total, however they may vary in detail. This is an example of a non-related cost basis since the amount of the contribution is not tied directly to costs.

When thinking in terms of maximising a contribution, remember that there may be other considerations to be taken into account, such as building a market on a long-term basis, keeping loyal customers, or even keeping your labour force in work, which will possibly reduce the maximum contribution you would like.

Your contribution from exports will, therefore, in each case be what is left after you have paid in full all your variable costs for labour and materials, a proportion of your general fixed costs, and any specific fixed costs incurred in obtaining that particular piece of business. That contribution should, as far as possible, be equal to the contribution made on your domestic market in total, since you should aim for equal contributions from both sides of your business.

If you wish to make comparative evaluations, remember to ignore all general fixed costs, and base your calculations on your total revenue, less specific fixed costs and all variable costs. You can do this to compare individual export markets as well as to compare domestic and overseas business.

Marginal selling

Many people hold that the way to export is to sell at marginal prices, that is, by ignoring your fixed costs on the basis that they have been fully accounted for in your domestic prices, and merely taking into account your variable costs, consisting of the labour and materials used in producing the goods. Provided that these are accounted for, then for any price at which you sell higher than the variable costs, you are producing some contribution to revenue. If you are over-produced or have unused capacity, it is a way of disposing of your extra production, but I suggest it is not a good way to regard exports, because you are not taking them seriously, nor are you making them contribute as much as possible to your revenue, because you have based these marginal prices on only part of your total costs.

There are, however, special circumstances when selling at marginal prices which can be justified in overseas markets, and I suggest the criteria should be, first, that you only export to a part of the world where you do not already export, and where you are unlikely to export, so that the marginal prices, which will be lower than your normal prices, cannot affect normal sales. Second, you must not in any way add to your fixed costs, either on a general or a specific basis. If you do incur any additional costs in selling, then you must add these to the additional variable costs concerned. Third, you should regard this as opportunist business. And fourth, you should establish that there is nothing better that you could be doing with the money.

You are certainly liable to come across the marginal buyer, who usually wishes to buy a fairly large quantity of goods, and is prepared to pay, say, 15 per cent below your normal export prices, and take delivery at your convenience. Should he require the goods more quickly you should make it clear he will have to pay the full price.

There is no reason why you should not take advantage of such opportunities, provided the criteria I have suggested are fully met. If your export sales are down, and you do not wish to manufacture for stock, an expensive business in these days, then you can quite properly resort to marginal selling. But you should be quite clear what you are doing, and that you are not making the maximum contribution to revenue from your exports that you should. The great bulk of your sales overseas should be costed in full and sold at prices which cover all fixed, variable and semi-variable costs, yet still make a reasonable contribution to revenue. Otherwise I suggest that it is not worth your while to export.

An example of successful marginal selling was that of a small company making novelty watches for children for export to Commonwealth countries. At a time when sales were temporarily depressed, a buyer for a chain of stores in Venezuela, where the company had never exported, offered the company a sizeable order provided they were given a 25 per cent discount. The company were thus enabled to keep their labour force fully employed; they made a contribution to revenue of 5 per cent after paying all additional variable costs, with no addition to their fixed costs; and they obtained business they would not otherwise have been given. It did not in any way affect their normal export business, and was not in fact repeated. But it had been worthwhile doing and that is how I suggest you view marginal selling.

An export price policy

So far we have considered our costs in some detail, and we have decided the revenue we expect to receive, along with the contribution to revenue we expect from exports, so the next step is to determine the basic price at which we will sell.

What should concern you most is to know what price the buyer will pay, that is the ultimate buyer or user, because the goods will generally pass through several hands (covered more fully in Chapter 5). While it is not always easy to discover the price a buyer will pay, you will almost certainly find that these prices vary in different parts of the world, because the factors influencing a purchase will not apply in the same way.

The factors are, first, the demand for the goods. Suppose you wish to export handmade sweaters. Do people want handmade sweaters or are they prepared to buy machine-made ones, or even go without sweaters altogether? Second, what value do the possible buyers place on the sweaters and how much are they prepared to pay for them? Third, how does the price of your handmade sweaters compare with other handmade sweaters available to the buyers? Fourth, is there any reasonable alternative to the sweaters; for instance, would a leather jacket be a reasonable substitute? Fifth, do the buyers have the means of buying handmade sweaters; and last, are there other things they need more, and on which they would prefer to spend their money?

If you apply these factors to buyers around the world, you will almost certainly find that the answers will be different. For example, the rich in Palm Beach, Florida may well be prepared to pay a higher price than the rich in Switzerland, because the former are less cost conscious than the latter.

Many people in Oslo may desire the handmade sweaters but not buy them because they have a better use for their money.

These considerations apply equally to industrial and consumer goods, because a factory owner in Spain may have the same need for some equipment as his opposite number in Singapore, but be unable to pay the same price for it. They also apply to services. There may well be a demand for education in Ghana, but that country would be unable to pay as high a price for it as her neighbour, the Ivory Coast.

It is therefore apparent that, if you have the same price for your goods or services all over the world, you may lose business because your price is too high, or you may lose profit because your price is too low, and that is just as much a loss as not getting the business. Yet you may feel that having to work out a special price for every customer will involve too much work to make the exercise profitable. It rather depends on how many things you sell and to how many different countries. I have suggested that, as a small company, you should concentrate on as few parts of the world as possible, so you may find that it is entirely practicable, as well as profitable, to quote different prices according to where you are selling, as well as in what quantity, at what time and according to when you will be paid.

Customs officials are generally suspicious of discounts, so try to quote firm gross prices, even though you may have allowed for discounts. You will not usually be allowed to sell at less than your domestic prices as most countries are not prepared to allow 'dumping', but it is unlikely that it would be worth your while to do so.

Quotations

Having arrived, subject to a consideration of your specific fixed costs, at a basic factory price or prices, you must now consider how you will quote these prices, which means deciding which of the accepted international terms of delivery you will use. These inform the buyer what is included in your price, when and where delivery of the goods takes place, and when the goods pass into the possession of the buyer, who is then responsible for them. They also define the duties of both the seller and the buyer in each case.

There are several of these terms of delivery, which have been defined and codified by the International Chamber of Commerce under the heading of 'Incoterms'. They define precisely what each term means, so when using one or other of them you should add 'Incoterms 1990' to your quotation. This new edition (which replaces the 1980 version) has been produced to reflect the major technological changes in international trade practice since 1980, particularly the growth of multi-modal transport at the expense of more conventional services.

Because in the past there have been a number of disputes as to the division of costs between buyer and seller, Incoterms 1990 now includes a section for each term, setting out these costs.

In addition, some out-of-date or little-used terms such as FOA (Free on Aircraft) and FOR (Free on Rail) have been dropped. The new exporter should obtain a copy of Incoterms 1990 from the International Chamber of Commerce, and note that the most commonly used terms are now as follows:

EXW (Ex works)
The basic quotation, which means the buyer must collect the goods from the seller, and pay all the transport and insurance costs from the time he takes over the goods at the seller's warehouse. The seller must, however, provide an invoice for the buyer.

FOB (Free on board)
This is now only to be used for shipments by sea, and of course needs to be qualified by the addition of the port to which delivery will be made by the seller, eg FOB Southampton. The seller, in addition, pays all loading charges on to the ship, as well as port charges, and provides the buyer with all the necessary documents including the Bill of Lading. The buyer takes over all risks, paying the freight and insurance from the time the goods go 'over the side of the ship's rail'.

FCA (Free carrier)
This should now be used for air, road and rail transport in place of FOB, especially where multi-modal container deliveries are used on a door-to-door basis. The seller must hand over the goods to the carrier at the point named by the buyer, where the responsibility passes to the buyer. All charges and documents up to that point must be paid for and provided by the seller.

CFR (Cost and freight)
This should now only be used for conventional maritime freight. The seller pays all FOB charges and freight to a named

56

destination, but the seller is responsible for insurance. The risk passes to the buyer as the goods go over the side of the ship's rail.

CPT (Carriage paid)
This is the equivalent for non-maritime transport of CFR, and is to be used particularly for road or multi-modal transport. The seller pays all freight charges to a point agreed between buyer and seller as the destination of the goods, and the risk passes from seller to buyer when the goods reach the first carrier.

CIF (Cost insurance freight)
As with CFR this should only now be used for conventional maritime transport, and is similar to CFR except that the seller pays the insurance charges. These should be based on the CIF cost plus 10 per cent, but only basic cover is stipulated. Hence a buyer may insist on some form of 'All Risks' when buying on this basis.

CIP (Carriage and insurance paid)
This is the non-maritime equivalent of CIF and the same care should be taken by a buyer, especially of manufactured goods, that the seller insures against all the risks the buyer wishes.

DDP (Delivered duty paid)
DDU (Delivered duty paid)
These two Incoterms can be used for any form of transport, and they clear up some confusion which arose when DDP was first introduced, regarding the payment of duties and local taxes etc. Now a seller may quote DDP if he wishes to give his buyer a truly delivered price. It is therefore the exact opposite of Ex Works. If, however, the seller wishes to pay only some of the local charges he may quote DDU and specify the charges he will pay.

Choosing Terms
Normally you quote as the customer requests, and you add on to your basic price and extra costs as required by the terms of delivery. If none are specified most exporters will probably choose either FOB or FCA because it gives them a good deal of flexibility in delivery, while many buyers like being able to save foreign currency by handling their own transport and insurance. But for delivery to the Community it is likely that DDP will become the most widely used Incoterm.

Currency

Your next problem is to decide whether you will quote in your own currency or that of your customer. Sterling is easier for you, and avoids your taking any exchange risk, since it is the customer who has to buy sterling to pay you. On the other hand, if he is not prepared to take this risk he may ask for a quotation in his own currency, so he knows exactly what he is going to pay for the goods. In this case you should be prepared to comply, and in order to avoid the risk of receiving less than you anticipated (because the rate of exchange goes against you) you make a contract with your bank to sell the foreign currency forward, and it is this rate that you use in your quotation. The mechanics of this transaction are explained in Chapter 9. It should be stressed that local currency quotations are much better for importers, and you should make them whenever you can.

You must also decide for how long the prices you quote remain operative, either by giving a definite date, or by stating that prices will be those ruling on the date of despatch. The latter is not so satisfactory, especially as many importers use quotations to obtain import licences or foreign exchange, and these are usually granted for exact amounts. When the goods arrive, if the prices are higher than the quotation, the importer may well have trouble in paying for them.

You make quotations, either by having a price-list, or by stating the details on a pro forma invoice, and if you quote ex works, FOB or FCA you should include details of the weights, measurements and packing of the goods, along with estimated freight and insurance charges. If you are tendering for supplies you will probably have to use a special tender form, which you may have to buy, and on it set out all the details asked for by the buyer.

Conditions of sale

Finally, to your quotations you will add your conditions of sale. You will almost certainly have these for your domestic business, but for exports you should make sure the following are included: your normal method of payment, dealt with in Chapter 8; a 'reservation of property' clause which retains your patent and other property rights; a statement to the effect that weights and measurements are supplied for transport purposes and are not part of the contract; that delivery dates are given in good faith; that damaged or defective goods will be replaced free of charge; and that you hold your customer responsible for obtaining any necessary import licences.

Orders

As you doubtless know, a quotation is an invitation to make an offer to buy, and the order is, therefore, the first part of the contract. Experience has shown that the quotation must be complete in all details, and the order likewise. If it is not, then any point not specifically covered must be queried with the buyer before the order can be accepted. Never make assumptions about orders from overseas, because this is where subsequent disputes nearly always arise. Because a customer normally buys on FOB terms it does not mean that he will in every instance. Because a customer usually arranges his own insurance it does not mean he always will. So always have in writing every relevant detail, and do not hesitate to query anything not specifically stated. If you have an order from a confirming house (Chapter 5) make sure you know who will be responsible for shipping the goods and who will pay you, as well as ascertaining that the confirming house has the authority to act on behalf of its principals.

Carrying out your part of the contract is the performance, and you should know exactly what this entails on your part. This means you should be familiar with both the Sale of Goods Act 1979, and the Uniform Laws of International Sales 1967, and the Uniform Laws on the International Sale of Goods.

Remember that you will be dealing with customers in other countries who may have an imperfect knowledge of English, and who may interpret things in a different way from you. They may even be out to cheat you, since Britain does not have a monopoly of the rogues in the world.

Chapter 5

To Whom Shall I Export?

You will need to know a good deal about your export customers if you plan to vary your export prices, as has been suggested in Chapter 4. Many people hold that you start exporting by deciding on the countries you wish to tackle. I suggest you would be better advised to choose a group of people or companies, and try to sell to them irrespective -- within certain limitations -- of the countries in which they live. There is, after all, no such thing as a 'market'. People talk about the Swiss market or the American market, but they do not exist. Suppose you sell handmade sweaters, then the markets in these countries will consist of a number of Swiss or American people able and willing to buy the sweaters. It is these people who are important to you, rather more than the fact that they live in Switzerland or the USA. So I suggest you forgo using the word market, and think first in terms of customers and then the countries where they happen to be.

Customers, consumers and users

For the sake of clarity you should try to distinguish between customers, consumers and users, because the terms are too often used with little clear indication of what is meant by them. The word 'customer' in export is best used for a person or company who orders from you, to whom you deliver the goods, and who pays you for them.

It follows that these customers will be the actual users in some cases. For example, a Brazilian manufacturer who buys a piece of machinery to make textiles will be the user of the machinery, so he could be classed as a customer and a user. However, an Italian importer of cotton yarn may not use it to make cloth, but resell it to textile manufacturers to use, in which case, if you were the exporter of the yarn, you would be dealing with a customer who would not be the user. Hence, for industrial goods and raw materials, your customers may be the users, or they may only be the buyers, and resell to the users.

In the case of consumer goods and consumer durables it is unlikely that the importer, that is your customer, will be the user or the consumer, because he will probably sell the goods to others to resell to the final users or consumers. And in many cases these people may be quite far removed from the original importer, to whom you as an exporter would sell. I suggest that you use the words 'consumer' or 'user' solely for those people who actually use or consume the goods.

If you sell services, the person who buys them from you is more likely to be the user of them, but it is customary in most cases for such people to be termed clients. If you sell skills, and not goods, it is customary to refer to the buyers as licensees, franchise holders or franchisees.

The reason why the distinction between these words is important is that you must first decide to whom you will physically sell your goods. Next, you must decide what distribution channels, if any, they will pass through on their way to the final consumer or user. Third, you must decide to which of these people you should direct your selling efforts. We are therefore concerned with two functions, that of distribution overseas and selling overseas, and while we are not considering in this chapter *how* to sell, we are concerned with deciding to whom to sell.

Groups of users and consumers

It is probably better to consider first the users or consumers because they will, to some degree, determine the type of customers to whom you should export, and from whom the users and consumers will draw their supplies.

Suppose you sell ceramic tiles, then it is likely that you will have at least two kinds of users, one being households buying tiles for use in homes where the tiles will be mainly decorative, and the other factories and commercial buildings using the tiles for reasons of heat or cleanliness. So to persuade people to buy your tiles you have to influence the householders in the first place, and those responsible for the factories and commercial buildings in the second place. Moreover, it is likely that the customers to whom you as an exporter actually sell the tiles, will be different again, since domestic tiles will be supplied from stock to wholesalers and retailers, while the industrial tiles may be bought by commercial interests direct from the exporter.

61

If you sell speciality foods, your consumers are not going to be the average households in any part of the world, but those who can both afford these foods and are concerned to have something out of the ordinary. They will not expect to buy them from normal food outlets, but from stores specialising in these unusual foods. Your customers will consequently have to use different channels of distribution.

You should, of course, already have a profile of your domestic users or consumers, and you then have to find their equivalents, as far as possible, in other parts of the world. You will need to list their main characteristics, such as the language they speak, their incomes, their buying habits and the reasons why they buy one article instead of another. You should try to find groups of users or consumers whose characteristics are as close to those of your domestic users or consumers as possible, because it is more likely that they will accept your goods. This will also help you to arrive at an acceptable price.

Drawing up a consumer profile

To illustrate how a profile of an exporter's customers can be built up, take the example of a small UK business making and selling temperature control systems used in factories. They tackled the West German factories and found that their customers insisted on three things: first, the control systems had to conform absolutely with all German technical specifications; they had to be completely reliable; replacement parts and service had to be available in West Germany. So long as the price was reasonable, price itself was not a major factor.

Second, the German customers did not wish to buy from a local distributor. They preferred to buy direct from the company in Britain, requiring all details of the systems in German, with prices quoted on a DDP basis in Deutschmarks.

Third, they wished for a German technical representative to call on them to explain the systems, but because of the regional character of the country they wanted a local representative from their own region. As a result, the UK company appointed several commission agents, who handle some two-thirds of all imports into West Germany.

The German customers claimed that they did not read direct mail, nor did they see any advertising for products such as these. Although there were three German competitors already selling similar systems, they were quite prepared to switch their purchases to the UK company, provided they were convinced the company was serious about selling to Germany. They judged this largely from whether or not they exhibited at the numerous trade fairs and exhibitions held in West Germany.

They proved to be solid, phlegmatic buyers who took time to make up their minds, and who demanded a great deal of time from the technical representatives. For this reason the commission agents had to be paid a higher rate of commission by the UK company than usual. It also took longer to sell to the German buyers than the exporters had anticipated.

This is a simplified example of how you draw up a profile of your customers overseas. When this company tackled the French factories they found that the profile was very different, and that they had to sell to customers whose needs were different and who reacted in a totally different way from the Germans.

You must then decide to which of these groups in various parts of the world you will try to sell, discarding those areas where imports are either forbidden or subject to barriers you cannot overcome. If you go on narrowing down the options, you should arrive at the groups of users or consumers with whom you are most likely to be successful, and it is on one or two of these that you should concentrate. The extent to which you become involved will also depend on the amounts you can reasonably supply.

To each group you will need to apply the social factors mentioned in Chapter 2, but you will find that these vary to a much lesser degree than you might imagine. So the tasks of persuading them to buy your goods will not be all that different from what you do with your domestic buyers, particularly because, as a small business, you will only deal with a few such groups, choosing those which are most similar to those at home.

Customers in the UK

You may feel that it is somewhat beyond the capabilities of your company to become involved with consumers and users overseas. Also, you may not wish to deal with the overseas customers who supply these consumers and users. This all means that either you would prefer to leave the actual exporting in the hands of others so far as this is possible, or you may feel that a compromise would be best, whereby you deal with a limited number of overseas territories, leaving the rest to others. If you decide that you wish to limit your dealings to customers in Britain, then you have several export opportunities to exploit, because there are many customers to whom you can sell without going outside the country.

Manufacturers

First, you can sell to other UK manufacturers, and leave them to export. A great deal of export trade is handled this way, and it is an option which suppliers of components could use. For example, if you made bicycle lamps you could sell these to bicycle manufacturers, and leave them to export the lamps along with the bicycles. You could, of course, extend your efforts later on to selling the lamps to bicycle manufacturers in other countries, leaving them to sell the complete bicycles in their own areas.

Confirming houses

Second, you may sell to overseas buyers with offices in Britain. Such offices are called confirming houses, which confirm the orders placed by these buyers to suppliers in the UK. The advantage here is that, not only do you not have to worry about shipping the goods overseas, since the confirming house usually arranges this, but also the confirming house will generally pay you in sterling as soon as you deliver the goods to them. Buyers overseas use confirming houses because of their expertise in finding suppliers, and for their ability to handle the shipping of the orders. They tend to specialise in buying unbranded goods, and are also used particularly when a large quantity of different goods is required. For example, a buyer in Australia may need several kinds of building components, and will ask a confirming house to arrange for a combined shipment of all of them at the same time, to save shipping costs.

The disadvantage of confirming houses is that you will have little means of influencing from whom they buy, nor will you be able to influence the overseas buyer, so that he specifies your goods on his order, in preference to your competitors'. At the same time there are some confirming houses which will act as agents for exporters and try to get their principals to buy their agency goods. For this they charge, but where they merely place orders the principal pays them for their services, so you are not involved in any costs other than supplying the goods.

Export merchants

Third, you may sell to export merchants, who buy for their own account and resell abroad where they have outlets or strong connections. These merchant houses are descendants of the merchant adventurers of Elizabethan times, and many of the names will be familiar to you, such as Paterson Zochonis, Jardine Matheson, the Borneo Company etc. They will attend to all the shipping, and pay you in Britain, so once again it is not difficult to supply for export.

There is, however, the disadvantage that you cannot easily influence what the merchant will buy. Moreover, since he has to resell, he will only buy what he knows he is sure to dispose of, so getting a new product into his hands is not easy. Nor can you easily influence the consumers or users overseas and thus force the merchants to buy from you, unless you are prepared to spend a good deal of money on promotion.

There is the British Exporters Association (BExA), formerly the British Export Houses Association (BEHA), and you should certainly see what these confirming houses and merchants can do for you, especially if you are just starting to export. There will, indeed, always be parts of the world you will not wish to spend time on, so this is a way to cover these areas.

Buying offices

If what you have to export is sold through department stores, you will find that many stores have their own buying offices in Britain. They place orders, ship them overseas and pay you here, so selling to them is no more difficult than selling to a UK buyer. Such buyers are always on the look out for something new, but once again you have little chance of influencing the users or consumers for whom the buying offices act. There is a list of such department store buyers available from the DTI.

Export concessionaires

You may, however, decide that you do not wish to become directly involved even with confirming houses, merchants or buying offices, in which case you could use the services of export concessionaires. They will either buy from you and resell for their own account wherever they can find buyers, or they will obtain orders for you to execute, and themselves attend to the shipping and documentation, in which case you would pay them an agreed rate of commission. Concessionaires operate either on a worldwide scale, or specialise in certain areas where they have good connections. One I know specialises in Middle East countries, and you might feel that dealing with the Arab world is a task better left to a concessionaire.

Crown Agents

There is one further organisation in Britain of which you should be aware, namely the Crown Agents. They are a public service working for principals in the public sectors overseas such as governments, transport authorities, power organisations, the armed forces, universities and schools in something like 50 countries. They buy anything from a power station to stamps and bank notes, and pay the suppliers in the UK, so are customers with whom you can safely deal.

Selling to any of the above customers will not involve you in travelling overseas, and while it may seem like exporting at second-hand so to speak, nevertheless for many small companies it may be the answer to export problems, particularly in the initial stages.

Overseas customers

If you are successful in obtaining some export business by selling to customers in Britain, you may well find that certain parts of the world seem to accept what you are exporting more readily than others. In fact, even among large exporters, most find that some 80 per cent of their business comes from a quarter of their markets. At this stage you should consider developing your exports in the one or two areas where sales are best.

What you will need is, first, some direct selling effort, which you may wish to employ others to do initially, because you do not have the resources at this stage to provide it yourself. Second, where the goods are going to pass through one or more hands until they reach the final user or consumer, you will require an efficient system of distribution. To achieve these you can appoint a local company to represent your firm in one or more parts of the world, and two kinds of local companies are available in most parts of the world.

Commission agents

If you sell industrial goods, or any goods where the importer is also the user, a commission agent may be appointed to obtain orders from the importers, these orders to be executed by the exporter, who will ship the goods and arrange to be paid for them by the importer. In return for the work of obtaining the orders, the agent will be paid a commission by the exporter. This will range usually from 2½ to 10 per cent of the value of the orders, the rate depending on the amount of effort that has to be put into getting the business.

As an exporter, you are protected to the degree that if you are sent no orders you pay no commission. Hence, the motivation for the commission agent is considerable, since he receives nothing if he does not sell. On the other hand, he risks no capital, nor does he usually take any credit risk, although you would expect him not to send you orders from customers who are not financially sound.

You will advise the commission agent of the prices and terms you are prepared to accept, and you may allow him margins of prices within which he must operate. It is customary for commission agents to be paid commission on *all* orders emanating from a territory, because it is likely that the commission agent will have had some hand in them, even though some importers prefer to send their orders direct to the exporter, and not via the agent.

You now have a direct representative in the country concerned; you have salesmen trying to get you business; you have an opportunity to set up an after-sales service; and you can obtain information as you wish, although you may have to pay for it. The two main disadvantages are that many commission agents take on too many principals, and can only afford to devote a small amount of time to each. As a small exporter you may suffer in this respect. Second, if you sell highly technical goods the salesmen may not know how to sell them, and it is difficult to keep them informed at a distance.

Distributors
When stocks need to be held locally, for supply to the local distribution channels, and the importer is unlikely to be the user or consumer of the goods, a distributor may be appointed. His tasks are first, to buy the goods from the exporter, then to pay for them, then to distribute them to the various channels of distribution, and finally to act as the exporter's representative in that part of the world.

As the exporter, you will sell your goods to the distributor on terms and at prices agreed between you. He will pay you for them and make his profit on the difference between his landed cost (the cost of the goods delivered to his warehouse) and his resale price, this being usually between 5 and 15 per cent.

You now have, not only a distribution process in action, but also a selling one, to the extent that the wholesalers and retailers who have bought from the importer will naturally try to sell the goods in order to get their money back. To protect the interests of the distributor, you normally appoint one only for a specific area, and do not supply any importer direct, but refer him to the distributor.

If a distributor cannot persuade wholesalers and retailers to take stocks of your goods, he may ask for stocks to be given to him on consignment; that is, they remain your property, and he will not pay you for them until they are sold. Consignment stock is sometimes the only way to obtain distribution, but it is not to be recommended because you are in effect financing the distributor, who has little incentive to sell. You will have to pay for storing the goods and their insurance, and you will lose money if they deteriorate. Moreover, you will have tied up your money in stock overseas, which will not please your accountant.

But for those of you selling consumer and consumer durable goods, having a distributor is an excellent way of becoming more involved with your customers, users and consumers than if you merely supply customers in the UK.

Finding and appointing commission agents and distributors

To find possible commission agents or distributors, first tackle the DTI and take advantage of their Export Representative Service, which will provide not only names but also status reports on the companies concerned. For each report you have to pay £25. Approach your local Chamber of Commerce, your own trade association and the international division of your bank. Look in the trade magazines of the country concerned; for instance, you will often see advertisements in the magazine *West Africa* from companies anxious to represent British firms. You may have in your files applications from such companies which you have not taken up. Even ask your friends and business associates if they know of anyone suitable. Make as large a list as possible.

Then write to all of them stating exactly what you require from them, what you can offer, and asking if they are interested. If so, suggest they give as many particulars about themselves as possible. This will weed out many of them, but with any luck you should be left with a short list of interested parties.

You must then visit them personally to find the most suitable. I appreciate this may not be easy for a small company, but from experience I can confirm that to appoint someone to represent you overseas from correspondence alone is almost certainly a recipe for failure. You may be able to join a trade mission to reduce the cost, but go you must.

As well as interviewing them, enquire into their standing with the trade, their financial standing, and their ability to sell. Good commission agents and distributors are hard to find, especially as the best ones may already be working for your competitors. Above all, you should feel you are able to work with them, because you will need to trust them implicitly to further your interests.

Agency agreement

If you are successful in finding an agent, you must conclude a formal legal agreement with him. This should be as short and simple as possible but contain the following essentials: a definition of the territory involved; for instance, does Malaysia include Brunei and Sarawak? The duties of each side must be stipulated, and the terms under which each party will do business. The financial conditions for both parties should be stated, especially how payments are to be made and what these cover; if you require additional work in the form of research or reports, how is this to be charged? You normally start with a trial period of six months, after which the agreement stands until cancelled by either side, but you will need legal advice here, because in many countries there are laws governing the contents of agency agreements. The Institute of Export has an excellent booklet on this subject, and you will want any such agreement checked by your legal advisers.

All this takes time, so allow anything up to two years to conclude such a deal, but it is worthwhile if out of it all comes a profitable working arrangement. You must help the local people all you can. You should visit them regularly, and provide as much information as possible. Set sales targets and be prepared to offer bonuses for achieving them. In fact, you will get out of such arrangements more or less what you put into them, and unless you are prepared to do a lot of work, do not bother to make them at all.

Company representatives

As a small business, you are unlikely to wish to set up a local sales or manufacturing company even in your best overseas markets, but you may well feel that having commission agents or distributors to obtain business for you is not very satisfactory, because you do not get as much of their time as you would like, nor are they expert enough at selling for you. If this is so, why not use your own salesmen to do the selling, especially if you sell technical goods? When you stop to think of it, sending a salesman around northern Europe, for example, is not going to be all that more expensive than sending him around Britain. Moreover, this will involve the company far more directly in export, and there is every reason to treat the European Community as one area in which to sell, especially from 1992 onwards.

Since you will probably not develop any special area until you have some export sales revenue, extending visits further afield may not be as daunting as it looks at first sight. It does not cost all that much to visit North America, or even African countries. You have the advantage that importers like to see people from the suppliers, and are often prepared to place larger orders as a consequence. If you already have a commission agent or distributor, the salesman can help them, so you do not need to disturb good existing arrangements.

I know a small company which sells pumps all over Europe with the part-time help of one of its domestic salesmen. I know a company selling knitwear in the USA which sends one woman out there twice a year. If you make the most of trade missions, you will be surprised how cheaply you can do it yourself.

Local channels of distribution

For those of you who sell consumer or consumer durable goods, there will be the problem of knowing through which local channels your goods pass from your customer, the importer, right down to the final user or consumer. You will need to see that the goods pass through these local channels effectively, and you will also have to know how your original prices to the importers are affected by the margins added along the way, so you can arrange that the price the user or consumer pays is in line with that charged by the competition.

Every part of the world will have a different pattern of local distribution, and this will vary according to the type of goods being sold. It would be impossible to give examples of all these, but the points you should bear in mind are, first, that the functions of wholesalers and retailers are in some countries merged with those of the importers, so you have companies who do some importing, some wholesaling and some retailing; Malta is a good example of such a country. In others the functions are more on the British lines.

Second, you will often find the names given to different channels vary, and that what may be sold in a chemist shop abroad, for example, is not the same as may be sold in a chemist in Britain. In Belgium, pharmacies sell medicine whereas beauty shops sell cosmetics. In Sweden, all liquor is sold in government liquor stores; there are no off licences as we have. In most developing countries, these distinctions are less marked, and most consumer goods are sold in what we would consider general stores. Moreover, such stores are little more than sheds in many African countries, the goods being kept in their packing cases, which may cause you to consider what type of packing cases you should use. And many consumer goods are sold by street vendors in country areas.

As an example of these local distribution channels, if you wished to obtain a share of the auto aftermarket, which is what the Americans call the accessories and spare parts market for vehicles, and worth some £16,000 million a year, you would need to know the following.

The manufacturer or importer supplies the warehouse distributor, known as a WD. He in turn sells articles to the jobber, or middleman (you will come across jobbers frequently in the US market). From the jobber, the goods go to the repair man who is the actual user, although the owner of the vehicle is the final purchaser. The repair man may be a service station mechanic, an independent mechanic or even a DIY motorist. Over and above this distribution system are the hardware stores, department stores and what are called variety stores, selling these spares and accessories. Should you wish to obtain a share of this market you would need a distributor, or even set up your own sales office, to ensure that the goods finally arrived in the user's hands.

A trade mission provides a good opportunity for you to study local channels of distribution, while the DTI will always provide essential information for specific trades in various parts of the world. You will, of course, have experience of the distribution channels in your domestic market, so all you really need to know is how far the local ones differ, and then act accordingly.

International agencies

You have already seen the work of the Crown Agents in Britain, but you should also be aware of the international agencies which have offices in other parts of the world, because they do buy goods of all kinds, and often in quantities well within the capacity of the small company, as I know from experience. The three most important are, first, the various agencies of the United Nations, such as the World Health Organisation (WHO), the Food and Agricultural Organisation (FAO), the United Nations Industrial Development Organisation (UNIDO), and so on. You can find out where these agencies are located from the United Nations Commission in London. The great advantage of selling to them, and they all buy a surprisingly wide variety of goods, is that they will usually do the shipping, and will pay you from their international funds.

Second, there is the Organisation for Economic Co-operation and Development (OECD) headquartered in Paris, consisting of most of the richer countries, who are concerned to help developing nations as far as possible. They also pay in international currencies.

Third, there is the Commonwealth Secretariat, to which all members of the Commonwealth belong, with various technical agencies helping the poorer members with equipment and aid.

The DTI has a special World Aid Section which will give you advance information on these kinds of contract.

Selling services

Although reference in this chapter has been to goods, those of you who sell services will generally deal direct with the users who, as I have said, are usually called clients. You will probably need to undertake selling efforts yourself to the overseas clients. If you are in a civil engineering company then you must bring it to the notice of likely clients, such as local or national authorities, building contractors etc. You can also offer the services to the international agencies and the Crown Agents.

There is one area of increasing importance, and that is the growth of consortia, or groups of people concerned with major projects such as the building of hospitals, hotels, universities, schools, factories, airports, dams and so on. The demand for the consortia comes about because the authority initiating the programme wishes to deal with one body who is then made responsible for the whole project. It often goes further than that, because there may be a need for an initial feasibility study before the project is started, while some projects need international financing. A consortium therefore requires a great many services, and if you can join one, your services will automatically be used.

You should, by now, be able to define clearly to whom you should export (that is, your actual customers), who will be the users or consumers of the goods, and whom you must persuade to buy because they, in the final analysis, will be the people paying for your goods or services, whether or not they pay you, as an exporter, direct. How you can set about selling overseas will be dealt with in Chapter 6.

Chapter 6
How Can I Sell Overseas?

Irrespective of how you arrange the distribution of your goods overseas, your next task will be to persuade your users and consumers to demand your goods in preference to those of your competitors. You can do this personally, or by using various methods of promotion, depending on whether you wish to work on your customers (who may or may not be users) or your consumers. As a small company, you will not be able to spend large sums of money on promotion, so the emphasis here will be on how to obtain as much selling effort for as little expenditure as possible.

Personal selling

While you can only sell personally to comparatively few customers, you will inevitably have to put in some personal selling. You will be well aware of the selling techniques which are usable anywhere in the world, albeit with some variations according to the environment in which your customers operate.

Dealing with shipping queries

Whenever you visit a customer overseas remember that your main problem will be to deal with his queries regarding the shipment of the goods, and that only when this has been dealt with to his satisfaction, will he consider placing another order. This is because so few exporters give a really efficient service in this respect. Many exporters fail in that they send salesmen overseas who have but a sketchy idea of what is involved with the transportation of goods, and the documents needed for this purpose, so they are unable to solve the many problems that arise and therefore are often unable to obtain any business.

As a small business you must not make this mistake, but make sure that whoever goes overseas in search of business is fully aware of all the transport and documentation problems which may arise, described in Chapter 7.

Dealing with payment problems

Anyone selling overseas is going to be more concerned with payment than a salesman at home because, as shown in Chapter 8, getting paid is more often closely connected with the delivery of the goods. Moreover, he will be concerned with when the customer is likely to pay for them, so he must set off armed not only with the various prices he will charge, but also the variations to these prices according to both the method of payment agreed, and the length of time before he receives the money. You cannot, when you are thousands of miles from home, easily call up and discuss these points, so the salesman will have to take these decisions himself, which means he must go fully prepared.

Customers overseas, of every nationality, have become extremely sophisticated in their buying from exporters, and a highly professional approach is necessary.

The time factor

There is a time factor in selling overseas which varies considerably in different parts of the world. For example, if you sell in India or Pakistan, or any eastern part of the world, time is elastic, the difficulty being to know how long you can afford to hang about waiting for a buyer to make up his mind. I once spent a whole day in a grubby Bombay bazaar while my customer debated the merits of a pseudonym for a lottery. I was tempted more than once to get up and walk away, but patience had its reward when, in the late evening, he gave me a large order.

Do not be surprised when you are making a sales pitch in a Middle East country if there is a constant flow of people in and out of the room. They are there to size you up, and help your customer decide whether he wishes to do business with you at all, before he considers the merits of what you are selling.

On the other hand, selling in North America requires you to put over your sales story within minutes, and everything will hang on these few minutes. Selling in Holland will require endless patience as the Dutch consider every angle of what you have said, and haggle over every cent. So whereas you can take your time in some countries, in others you will have little time to take.

Local characteristics

Buying characteristics often vary according to nationality. In Italy, for example, you will need to be dramatic, because life is a series of dramas, as it tends to be in France or Greece. In Germany you need a methodical, calm approach, as you would adopt in German Switzerland.

The venue for doing business varies, and you must become accustomed to using cafés in Spain, for instance, because many buyers do not have offices, but frequent certain cafés, where the sellers queue up to see them, each buyer having a favourite café which you must get to know. Buyers in Sri Lanka sit at the entrance to their warehouses, and you will be fortunate if you are offered a chair. Usually you stand in the street, which is off-putting for a salesman used to well furnished offices. Do not be misled by the appearance of offices when they exist. In many countries, especially in South America, tax is levied not on figures (which are notoriously inaccurate) but on the appearance of the company, so the owner uses an office with the paint peeling off the walls, and holes in the ceiling, in order to minimise his taxes. I once did more business in such a place in a seedy suburb of Lima, than I did in the smarter offices in the centre of the city. Nor are the appearances of buyers any guide to their ability to buy. The Malaysian dealer who looks as though he has almost nothing to spend turns out to have millions in the bank.

Inducements

Another difficult factor you will have to contend with is that of inducements, or bribery if you prefer. It exists everywhere in the world, but it seems more blatant abroad because the inducement is usually required in hard cash. At the same time it is, as someone remarked, more honest because there is nearly always a 'rate for the job'. You must make up your own mind whether to pay an inducement or not, and if so to make an allowance for it in your costs. My own feeling is that it is not for me to sit in judgement on local customs, and so long as the customer ultimately pays, then I will go along with the system, but only after the order is placed, and never before. You have to remember that many people are badly paid and that an inducement is looked on as part of their salary. But do formulate a clear policy which your company will adopt, and decide whether to go along with inducements, or to leave that kind of business alone.

Planning overseas visits

All selling visits overseas must be costed in advance and clear objectives set in terms of the revenue likely to be obtained from them. There is no way a small company can afford to send people around the world unless the costs will be recovered sooner or later.

When planning such visits take into account public holidays, and the weather. Do not try to sell in Trinidad in carnival time, while avoiding public holidays in South American countries can be a real headache. The DTI booklets 'Hints to Exporters' give much valuable information on this point.

Visitors from overseas

Instead of going to visit buyers in their own country you can encourage them to visit you, partly because you can show them the company and what you make, and partly because this helps you to involve the whole company in export. Over and over again, companies who are successful exporters maintain that their success is due to all their personnel being concerned with exports, and being able to meet export customers. It is far better if people know the person to whom the exports are being despatched rather than their merely being a name in some far off place. Another way of having people come to see you is to be involved with those on inward missions to this country, these missions being sponsored by the DTI, who provide financial help for the organisers. So offer the DTI your company's facilities in entertaining these visitors.

Promotion budgets

Although British exporters have gained a not undeserved reputation for insufficient promotion of their goods and services, I trust this criticism will not be levied at small companies, because they know that goods and services simply do not sell themselves. People will not buy goods from another country in preference to locally made products, nor will they buy from a totally unknown company, unless they are persuaded so to do.

The amount of money which a small business can afford to spend will of necessity be limited, but the amount must be arrived at in a logical way. This means forgetting about conjuring a number out of the air, and doubling or halving it, or deciding that you will spend the same, or more or less, than last year.

77

Clearly there must be some relation between the revenue you hope to gain from your export sales, and the amount of money that has to be spent to obtain that revenue, which is why many companies work on a percentage basis. That is, they allow in their costs for x per cent to be spent on promotion, and arrive at the figure either from past sales in the country, or from anticipated sales. The first problem is to decide the percentage, and figures vary from 1 to 70 per cent. The second problem is to decide what to do with small promotional budgets generated in this way. The third difficulty is that because you have earned so much promotion allowance, or hope to earn that amount, it does not mean you should spend it. Moreover, if you wish to open up a new country you will have earned nothing to date, or the percentage will be too small for the initial effort. By all means have some sort of percentage in mind, according to how competitive your prices are and what are your costings, but that percentage should be elastic and not rigid.

It is better, I suggest, to arrive at a promotion budget by forecasting what it will cost you to obtain a certain revenue from a particular part of the world. Then decide if that amount of business is worth having from a point of view of its contribution to your revenue. This must be seen in relation to how much you can actually afford to spend, and as your exports grow, you may well find that a fairly similar percentage figure emerges for each part of the world. But you should start as I have suggested, and then arrive at a promotion budget which represents a reasonable amount for the company to risk, as a means of obtaining a revenue which will produce a certain contribution.

In Chapter 10 a marketing plan is considered for a small company exporting hand tools principally to Kenya, Zambia and Malaysia. It is suggested that they should allocate £5000 to promotion, to achieve a total revenue of £100,000, producing a gross revenue of £25,000 after production and other costs. How was this £5000 arrived at?

The company, as you will see, decided that they needed to spend some money in each of the three countries on advertising in the local technical publications, and the cost was estimated at £2500. It was also decided that, to obtain the estimated sales, visits would be needed to each country, the estimated cost being £2500. Hence the £5000 promotion budget, a specific fixed cost allocated to these countries. Was it a justifiable cost?

After deducting this £5000 from the gross revenue of £25,000 the contribution to the company's revenue is £20,000. This as you will see represented a return of 25 per cent on the capital employed, which was felt to be satisfactory. The £5000 also represents an expenditure of 5 per cent on the total revenue from sales. This also is a reasonable amount to spend on this type of goods. Industrial products will generally require between 1 and 10 per cent of sales on promotion, while fast moving consumer goods will generally require much larger amounts, anything between 10 and 50 per cent, but you are unlikely to be involved with that scale of expenditure.

So work out how much you think is needed to produce the sales expected, and then check the ratio of expenditure to revenue to see that it is roughly in line with what your sales will produce on a percentage basis. If you are tackling new export areas for the first time, you may need to spend more to become established, but in this case I suggest you treat this as a form of capital expenditure, and do not include it in your export budget figures.

As far as possible all promotion expenditure should be allocated to specific areas, and monitored to ensure that it is producing the results expected. If it is not, the expenditure must be adjusted accordingly. Much depends on the accuracy of your forecasting, but that will be covered in Chapter 9.

You will never have enough money to do all the promotion you would like, and will always be having to make decisions on the best possible use to be made of the limited money available, but this is the way to make the best possible use of the money. You will also find that you can never be sure what you got for your money, or whether you would have done better or worse if you had not spent it, or had spent twice the amount. But with experience you will find that you develop a kind of instinct which tells you if you are spending reasonably under all the circumstances.

Public relations

It may seem strange to start with this aspect of promotion, but as a small business, you are concerned to get as much publicity as possible for your company and its goods for the lowest cost, and this is one way of doing it.

The Central Office of Information is the government's main publicity body and their task is to help you obtain publicity overseas. They do this by sending out stories about British exports, with photographs, and having them published worldwide in newspapers and magazines. All you need to do is supply the information and illustrations. They also provide similar information for the BBC's external services, who publicise new developments in British industry.

If you wish to do more in areas where you are actively engaged in developing export sales, contact the DTI's Publicity Unit and ask them to provide you with the names of British based correspondents of overseas publications, to whom you can send material, and even invite them to come and see you and obtain an exclusive story for themselves. At the same time send details of your export successes to the DTI Publicity Unit, since they can often use the material for UK publications, and this may then be picked up overseas.

All you need is a small sum to cover the cost of the photographs and producing the stories. You can build on this basis by also sending the material to your customers, commission agents or distributors overseas, to encourage them in their efforts on your behalf.

You can capitalise on any visits you make overseas by informing the press of your visit when you arrive, giving them a brochure about your company, and your interest in their country. You can also offer to speak at functions of local Rotary Clubs etc, and publicise your company in that way. If you can establish yourself as an authority on your particular goods or industry, your views will be sought whenever an editor has need of comments, and this again provides you with the opportunity of getting publicity for the company.

When you have visitors from abroad, not only should they be introduced to all the members of the company, but you should advise the local press, television and radio stations, and offer them the chance of getting a story. Make sure the visitors are well photographed, and that copies are sent to them at home so that they can use the material locally.

None of this requires much money, mainly imagination and some ability to write and speak in public. But the results will far outweigh the costs, and every small business should be able to afford the small amounts involved.

Sales literature

You will almost certainly need some literature for export, as you do for your domestic trade. If possible, use the literature you already have in the form of leaflets, catalogues, instructions for use etc, although it may well have to be adapted to make it suitable for other countries.

First, the text will have to be in the appropriate language, for which you can use a translation agency. The DTI can provide a list of such agencies. But translation is a bad concept, since you need the words rewritten in the other language, rather than merely translated. Make sure you always have the local version put back, independently, into English to ensure the correct meaning has been retained. Do not use your secretary or a friend for this work, unless they are skilled writers. If you have commission agents or distributors they may help, although they also may not be capable of the original work. Try to stick to simple English for countries where it is appropriate, and avoid any play on words, which often have no local equivalent.

Multilingual literature may be used where a country requires more than one language, such as in Malaysia where English, Chinese and Malay will usually be necessary. Technical words often have no exact equivalents, and may require additional explanation.

Second, make sure the illustrations are appropriate, especially of people, because it is easy to show the wrong types. In Jamaica, for example, there are at least ten different colours, all typical of this multiracial society. If unsure, avoid people altogether, or show British people (as being neutral). But use simple illustrations, especially in instructions for use, since many machine operators overseas have an imperfect knowledge of English, and even of their own language.

It is a good idea to design literature for use at home and overseas at the same time, because words take up different amounts of space — German for instance requires some 25 per cent more than English — and if using Arabic, you will need to design the leaflet to read from right to left.

If you have all the literature printed in Britain you may save on printing costs, but incur duty when it is sent overseas. At least its production is under your control, provided you are using experienced and competent printers. Having it printed abroad saves duty, but you have less chance of spotting and correcting mistakes.

Be wary of excessive demands for literature from customers overseas, who have a habit of over-ordering, and make sure that its distribution is assured before it is produced. Otherwise you may find it languishing on shelves gathering dust, instead of being used, and that you cannot afford.

You will probably wish to send out some direct mail shots, and the DTI can provide the names of companies able to supply mailing lists, and carry out the mailing for you. Not all countries are suitable for direct mailing, since the postal service may not be effective, while the number of people with postal addresses may be limited.

You will, as time goes by, be able to build up your own mailing lists, and remember that the wastage associated with direct mail may be reduced if the mailing comes from Britain. Do not overlook Christmas and New Year greetings, but post early for Christmas which starts early in December in Europe, but later for the New Year which starts in February in the Far East. The value of these greetings is, as regards export, far greater than you might imagine.

Trade fairs and exhibitions

While the costs of taking part in major fairs and exhibitions overseas may seem formidable, the Fairs and Promotions Branch of the DTI specialises in helping exporters to participate at reduced rates, so that even small businesses should not find it impossible to use this form of promotion.

There is a joint venture scheme whereby a number of British firms can be helped to put on a collective presentation of British goods. There is the possibility of a British pavilion at an appropriate trade fair, where you can buy the exhibition space at a reduced rate, for example at the IM Fair at Cologne specialising in sweets and biscuits. The DTI often mounts all British exhibitions and store promotions with a British theme, where you get help not only with space costs, but with the transport of your goods and some of your own travelling costs.

While there are innumerable fairs and exhibitions taking place all over the world, you will choose only one or perhaps two in a year most suitable for your type of goods, and in the part of the world where you wish to try to sell them. The DTI will provide a list of the most important, while Lunn Poly not only issue a trade fair guide, but will also book all your flights and accommodation to them.

There are so many advantages to be gained from showing your goods at a trade fair. If you sell clothes for children, for example, what better way of testing the market than by exhibiting at the National Kids Fashion Show in New York?

Or going to the Miami Trade Fair to meet the USA store buyers? If you wish to break into COMECON countries an excellent way of meeting trade buyers is at the Leipzig Trade Fair. Not only can you sell; you can also check against the competition prices, competitive products and all the details of what you are selling. Try to display in an interesting and unusual way. For example, the small island of Barbados took a minute stand at Miami, but filled with several gorgeous local girls, and offered free rum punches to all and sundry. As a result they had more visitors than almost any other stand, and sold hundreds of people on the idea of a holiday in Barbados.

Make the most use of all the fair's own publicity services, and remember to keep a careful record of every worthwhile visitor, because it is the follow-up work you do that will bring the results. You must see that every visitor is contacted at regular intervals after the fair, since this is when the real orders will be placed.

You will need a plentiful supply of literature, and sufficient people to cope with the visitors in their own languages. You may have to pay duty on the goods you take, which you can either sell, or, if you bring them back, claim a refund of the duty paid.

Should you be unable to afford to take part in an official fair, you have the alternative of putting on a small exhibition of your goods in a hotel, as one small company did in Rotterdam. The total cost was a few hundred pounds, but they obtained orders worth a few thousands, which was the limit of their extra production capacity. You do not have to be large to be successful, and if Barbados can do it so well, so can you.

Advertising

While it is unlikely that, as a small business, you will wish to advertise on any major scale overseas, you may well find a need for a limited amount of advertising in selected countries.

Your first problem will be to decide how such advertising should best be handled. I suggest you do not allow this to be done by your local commission agents or distributors, if you have them, because experience has shown that joint advertising of this kind is nearly always a failure, as either you or the local people will gain the greater advantage. Moreover, you cannot expect the local people to contribute to the cost of advertising since they are paid to sell, and you can hardly expect them to give up part of their profits to advertise, unless such profits are too high. Therefore, I suggest that you should always be prepared not only to spend money on advertising yourself, but also, as this is your money, to control how it is spent.

You can book the space in overseas publications yourself, using the British representatives of the various publications (the Overseas Press and Media Association — OPMA — will provide a list) in which case you will also have to provide the material to be published, or you can use your domestic agency to do the work for you. In these days most agencies have learned how to handle advertising in overseas publications, and this is probably the better way to do it, particularly when the amount of advertising is likely to be modest.

Having decided whom you wish to influence, that is your customers, users or consumers, you must determine which section of the media available locally reaches these people most effectively and economically. Media patterns vary considerably overseas from those in Britain, but are not difficult to learn on the scale on which you are likely to advertise.

Some points about these patterns are, however, worth remembering. For example, if you export industrial goods and wish to advertise them in technical journals overseas, in many smaller countries you will find an absence of such publications. Hence, you may have to use the local newspapers, since these are what the local business people habitually read. In Middle East countries, for example, there are few if any good technical publications, but the local Arabic papers cover the local business community.

In other countries, where there are many technical publications, you have to be careful not to choose publications which claim extensive coverage but which in fact print few copies, and are read by few people, in spite of extravagant claims to the contrary. Remember you can advertise in the Soviet Union and other Eastern European countries in technical publications which is another way of influencing the state buyers there.

Consumer magazines, as you would expect, are plentiful in the more developed countries, but thin on the ground elsewhere, and even more so in countries with a high degree of illiteracy. Consequently, you will find that in some African countries, for instance, the ordinary magazines have a fairly limited coverage.

While we often tend to dismiss advertising in cinemas in Britain as being of doubtful value, in many parts of the world going to the cinema is still the main source of local entertainment. Open-air and drive-in cinemas attract large audiences in many countries in Africa, the Caribbean and the Far East, and you can put over a sales message quite cheaply by using cinemas on a selective basis.

A small business is unlikely to be able to afford radio or television advertising, which would of course have to be handled locally, but you may be tempted to use publications which claim to cover many countries, and thus save costs. While there are some which can justify their claims, there are many which are not read locally, only by visitors to embassies and high commissions on whose tables the publications usually lie, so be careful when considering them, although you can use a publication such as the *Economist* with safety because it is widely recognised and read nearly all over the world. News magazines such as *Time* or *Newsweek* are also read, and with local editions you can to some degree confine your expenditure to specific areas. *Reader's Digest* is another internationally owned publication with editions in most countries. A magazine such as *West Africa* covers most of the West African states. The *Financial Times* has a special European edition.

Make the greatest possible use of your customers when choosing media and get them to recommend the ones they think are best. When you are overseas yourself, check on what your customers read, and thus build up a picture of the media which seem best for you in a particular region. Then with the help of the British representatives of the publications, and your domestic agency, it should not be difficult to choose the correct publications for your goods.

Equally crucial will be what you say in your advertising, the theme being all-important. For example, it is no use stressing the labour-saving advantages of equipment in countries where labour is cheap, and local industry labour intensive. On the other hand, it would be advantageous to stress the ease of operating machinery where labour is largely unskilled. Whereas in North America, the stronger and more compelling your advertising the better, in many eastern countries, you must be less bombastic and adopt a certain amount of 'humility' in your advertising, because people in the east are not impressed by exaggerated claims. While you may use a fairly similar basic theme all over the world, it is the way it is presented that has to vary according to local idiosyncrasies.

This will mean altering the words used, as has already been

85

suggested when preparing sales literature. Headlines are often a problem, either because they do not easily translate into other languages, or because people are unused to terse statements which are common in Britain. Slogans are better avoided for the same reason. You must have the advertisement copy checked locally, so you can avoid making embarrassing mistakes, such as the company which used the wrong Swedish word for service, and claimed that they gave the same service to their customers as a bull gives to a cow, which was not quite what they intended.

Illustrations must also be checked, so the goods do not appear in unusual settings. Cartoon style drawings are easily misunderstood in many parts of the world, and are better avoided. Make sure your name and trade mark, if any, are prominent since they may be less familiar to people than the local competition.

In many countries overseas there is a rather less strict division between advertising and publicity in the editorial columns of the publications, which means that you can insist on some free editorial publicity if you are an advertiser. In many Central and South American countries you can buy editorial space, which means you can obtain publicity for a small outlay, certainly paying less than if you took large advertisements. Provided you use your wits and imagination, you do not always have to spend large sums on promoting your goods overseas.

Gifts and samples

You will almost certainly be asked for these, and you must decide whether or not to supply them. While they may be a waste of money for a small business, provided the gifts are fairly small, they can be a means of building up goodwill among customers, especially if the gifts bear some relation to the goods being exported. For example, a company making dustbins gave away miniature dustbins which were used on people's desks to hold paper clips etc. That company's name was never forgotten. You can present these gifts when you visit customers overseas, and you can give them to visitors from overseas when they come to see you.

If you can build up a reputation for always giving an annual gift you can impress customers, as Pirelli have done with their famous calendar. When I was selling Eno's Fruit Salt, we gave away an annual Eno diary which was much prized by customers.

Limit the distribution to customers or those agreeing to buy, and you will generate some publicity at a fairly reasonable cost, especially if you can produce your own gifts in the factory.

Samples are likely to be sold on the local market if they have been given away free, and I would suggest limiting the use of samples to specific occasions, at an exhibition or trade fair, or in a particular store promotion, for example. But in many parts of the world anything free has a much greater value than in the domestic market, and provided the amount you spend is kept within reasonably small limits, giving something away can create more goodwill among customers than you might imagine. There is a vogue today for wearing tee shirts, sweaters and ties, as well as carrying bags, all bearing the name of a specific product, and a small company could well capitalise on this trend, at no great cost to itself.

Chapter 7

What Transport Shall I Use?

Having obtained some export orders your task is now to arrange for the goods to be shipped to the customers in the quickest and most effective way. This assumes that you have been asked to arrange shipment, and that your customer has not specified the method. If he has sent instructions you must follow them; otherwise you decide the method of transport.

Methods of transport

The five most commonly used methods of transport in the export trade are as follows:

Sea

Most goods go by sea, because ships provide the cheapest method of transport. Ships can carry heavy and bulky loads. While it costs comparatively little to propel ships through the sea, they travel slowly. Moreover, if the customer is some way from the port, transhipment can add considerable additional time to the voyage. For example, shipping to Kampala in Uganda means a long haul from the port of Mombasa in Kenya. This time factor also adds to the risks of damage or loss to the goods. You will find details of the sailings in *Lloyd's Loading List*, while shipping lines send out sailing cards to exporters giving details of their next sailings. Most shipping lines are organised in conferences, which maintain regular services irrespective of the demand for cargo space.

One major development in sea transport has been the introduction of container ships; that is, ships specially built to carry containers. Because they spend less time loading and unloading their cargoes, this cuts down the length of time goods are in transit. When you ship your goods in containers, you either use a full container load, or, if you are only shipping a small amount of cargo, your goods go in the container along with those of other exporters. You deliver not to the sea port but to the container depot.

The other major development is the RoRo (Roll on/Roll off) ferries which mean you use road or rail transport in conjunction with sea transport as one operation.

Air

While some 75 per cent of the world's trade goes by sea, an increasing amount now goes by air, because it is quick, the goods require less packing, and stand less chance of being damaged or lost. Moreover, smaller quantities mean less of your money being tied up in stocks in transit. On the other hand, shipping by air is costly. It is limited to those goods which can be taken in an aircraft, and it is subject to delays due to bad weather.

Certain goods are most suitable for air transport, such as perishable food or flowers, highly seasonable goods, emergency supplies, quickly required spare parts, and even highly valuable goods which should remain at risk for the shortest possible time.

Booking space

Air cargo is carried on most passenger flights, as well as on all-cargo services which carry large, bulky or restricted consignments that would be unsuitable for transport on passenger planes. Space may be reserved for air cargo in the same way as passenger accommodation is booked.

Special arrangements are necessary in advance for valuable cargo, live animals, pieces of unusual shape and size, perishables and consignments requiring special care or attention in transit. When goods have to be transhipped, it is only necessary to make the special arrangements with the first carrier, who will pass on the instructions to transfer connections.

A legible and durable address must show on each part of the consignment, giving the consignee's name, street and city, as on the air waybill, which shows the contract terms. Instructions for carriage must be given in writing to the carrier.

Air parcels

Many airlines run a small parcels service (Swissair and Transworld, for example) to their country of origin; they offer overnight delivery.

Road

The main advantage of road transport is that it offers a door-to-door service. Across Europe goods move with minimum delays at frontiers. It is particularly useful for the small exporter because of its groupage system, whereby a freight forwarder can consolidate the shipments of several exporters, thereby saving freight costs, and at the same time providing a regular service to the main cities. It is less costly than air, and not much slower. Consult the Road Haulage Association for all aspects of moving goods overseas by road.

Rail
Throughout Europe the railways have developed a highly sophisticated network of cargo trains, made up of containers, privately owned wagons, and train ferry wagons organised on a groupage basis. Rail can be quicker than road, especially over longer distances, although it is not necessarily a door-to-door service. It is extremely reliable, and less subject to delays than air or road.

Parcels service
British Rail offers an express parcels service to 23 European countries (maximum weight 100 kilograms, unless a special arrangement has been made; maximum length 4 metres). The parcels must not include firearms, ammunition, dangerous goods, live animals, or high value items. The prices include documentation, handling and customs processing charges; delivery is charged extra for some countries; in Portugal or Turkey there is no delivery service. Collection in the UK can be arranged through City Link.

Parcel post
Frequently overlooked is the excellent service provided by the Post Office, all over the world, using surface or air transport. There are several specialised services such as the ASP (or Accelerated Surface Post) which uses a combination of air and surface transport.

There is Datapost, offering speedy delivery to specified overseas destinations. Items may be handed over post office counters, but for regular exporters, a door-to-door contract service is available. The service is limited to items acceptable by letter and parcel post, and contents are subject to the customs regulations of the country of destination. There are restrictions on size; the maximum weight is 15 kilograms except to Japan and Malaysia, where it is 10 kilograms.

Full details of all postal services abroad are to be found in the *Post Office Guide*, and in the Royal Mail *Overseas Compendium*.

Continental Express Ltd of Basildon offers a postal parcels service for exporters which includes free collection in the London postal area and customs clearance at destination.

Couriers

Courier companies specialise in personal deliveries, office to office or airport to airport, of small items such as documents, finished artwork, samples, spare parts, computer tapes, films, medicines, X-ray films, pharmaceutical and construction equipment. Some companies have countrywide networks in the UK; only the largest offer worldwide deliveries. Each company will have its own size and weight restrictions.

Freight rates

By sea

The conference lines have fixed tariffs, but if you always ship by a conference ship you will be entitled to a rebate of around 10 per cent. If you use a non-conference ship you will probably pay less, but have to bargain about the rate, and you lose the certainty of knowing when the ship will actually sail.

Except for very high value goods, sea freight rates are based on weight or measurement, whichever is the greater. This means you must weigh your goods in kilograms. You must also measure them, usually in centimetres, and then cube the result. The shipping lines compare the weight with the volume on the basis that 1 cubic metre equals 1 metric tonne. There are, as you know, 1000 kilograms in a metric tonne, while to turn cubic centimetres into cubic metres you divide by 1,000,000. Hence, goods measuring 3.2 cubic metres but weighing 2.8 metric tonnes would pay 3.2 times the freight rate. In practice, on this basis, most cargoes are larger than they are heavy. Rates vary according to destination and type of goods, while there is usually a minimum rate. Freight is normally payable in advance, and quoted in US dollars, which means there are often surcharges varying with the value of the dollar, and the cost of the fuel, also payable in US dollars (called the CABAF or Currency Adjustment Bunker Adjustment Factor).

By air

Air cargo rates are fixed by IATA, the International Air Transport Association, and there is little difference between the rates charged by different airlines. Since airlines are more concerned with weight than size, airlines use the ratio of 7000 cubic metres to 1 kilogram. This means that most consignments going by air are charged by weight, rather than by volume.

By road and rail

Rates for road transport are highly competitive, but rates by rail are standard, varying according to destination, type of goods, and the service used. The same ratio of weight to volume is used as for sea transport.

Since your aim is to transport your goods as quickly, effectively and cheaply as possible, deciding on the method of transport involves many considerations which will be examined in Chapter 9, since the choice of transport can affect the amount of money you make from your exports.

Export packing and marking

How you pack the goods will also affect your transport costs since there are special container rates, both for full container loads and less than full loads.

Export packing has become a highly specialised activity and you will be well advised to consult an export packing company if you have no experience of packing goods for export, or if you feel that some improvements could be made. This advice can be obtained also from the Packaging Division of the Research Association for the Paper and Board, Printing and Packaging Industries (PIRA).

The first factor you must consider is the liability of your goods to damage or loss. You will already have some experience in your domestic trade, but goods going overseas may be subjected to a great deal more handling than at home, and probably a good deal of rough handling especially when they need to be transhipped.

Second, the type of transport affects packing in that goods in a container should require less packing, although they can be damaged within the container if not adequately protected. Goods going by sea will probably require more packing than those going by air, while road transport may save packing, compared with rail transport which may increase the need for it.

Third, you must comply with any local customs regulations. For example, you are not allowed to use any wood packing materials when shipping goods to Australia, unless the packing has been impregnated and a certificate issued to that effect. The *Post Office Guide* gives details of prohibited and recommended packing materials where these apply.

You must take into account the climatic conditions to which your goods will be subjected, extremes of heat or damp being extremely detrimental to many types of goods.

You should also consider the resale value of the packing materials you use because these, in many parts of the world, will make your goods more attractive to the buyer, who can obtain additional profits by selling or using the packing. In a country such as India nothing is ever wasted, and imported goods are sometimes sold for no more profit than can be obtained from selling the cases in which they are packed.

If you sell dangerous goods, that is to say goods so classified by the DTI, which will conform with the International Maritime Dangerous Goods Code, not only will you need to specify these on a special form (Figure 7.2, page 103) to the transport authorities, but you will also need to pack and label them in accordance with the regulations, for which special labels must be used. There are also internationally accepted labels for fragile goods, to show which way up they must be stored etc (Figure 7.3, page 104).

When you ship by air, road, rail or parcel post you must mark the consignments with the name and address of the consignee, although you will not indicate the goods, to prevent theft. When you ship by sea, however, you should use the internationally acceptable method of showing no more than the order number, the destination, the name or mark of the consignee, and the number of packages in the consignment, an example being given below.

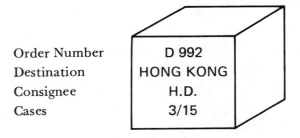

Order Number	D 992
Destination	HONG KONG
Consignee	H.D.
Cases	3/15

Figure 7.1 *Case markings*

This is because the goods will be delivered to the consignee by the airlines, road operators, railways or Post Office, whereas goods sent by sea will not be delivered to the consignee, so the marks are for identification purposes only, a point you should note because it will affect the documents used and the method of payment you can adopt.

It is customary also to indicate on the packages the weights and measurements in centimetres and kilograms, since this information will be needed by all the people concerned with transporting the goods, both here and inside the customer's country.

You have now assembled the basic information you will need to complete the documentation for transport and customs purposes, and it is worth making a note of this information as follows:

    The name, marks or address of the consignee
    The goods contained in the consignment
    The method of transport
    The route to be taken
    The number of the packages
    The marks on those packages
    Their weights in kilograms (and metric tonnes)
    Their measurements in centimetres (and cubic metres)
    The final destination of the goods.

One final point about packing, where you are sending a variety of goods in different packages in one shipment. You will not indicate the contents on the packages, but to enable your customer to identify the contents of each, you should include in your documents a packing list, set out as in Figure 7.4 on page 105.

Transport documents

By sea
Having assembled your basic information about a shipment overseas, you will use it on almost all the documents you have to make out, beginning with the booking form for sending goods by ship. While you can find out if space is available by phone, it is customary to confirm the details to the shipping line on forms such as those shown in Figure 7.5 on pages 106-7. Shipping lines have their own forms, or you can use a standard

shipping instructions form as shown.

The next form to be completed will be the *standard shipping note* (SSN), shown in Figure 7.6 on page 108. This must accompany all goods when sent to the docks, and having completed it, you keep one copy for your files and send the remaining five with the goods. One copy will then be returned to you without any remarks, if the goods arrive at the docks in the same condition as you have described them. The SSN, therefore, acts as a receipt for the goods from the port authorities. If there are any discrepancies the SSN will be amended, and you can then correct the mistake before the goods are shipped.

An SSN is also an instruction to the docks as to what to do with the goods, it being their responsibility to see that the goods are delivered to and loaded on the ship which you have designated. The third function of the SSN is to enable the port authorities to charge you for handling the goods, charges you have to pay if you are shipping under an FOB contract, or which you would invoice to the customer under an ex works contract for which you were arranging shipment.

After the goods have been loaded on to the ship, and the ship has sailed, the shipping line will eventually issue you with a *bill of lading*. In practice you may make this out yourself and have the shipping line sign it. There are several kinds of bills of lading but an example of a conventional one is shown in Figure 7.7 on page 109. Most shipping lines have their own bills of lading, but all are now to a fairly standard design on A4 size.

The bill of lading acts, first, as a receipt for the goods, and provided they are, as the bill says, 'In apparent good order and condition . . .', you will receive what is known as a clean bill. Should they be damaged or incomplete in some way, you will receive a 'dirty' or 'claused' bill, and the shipping line will not admit to any liability as to their condition when off-loaded. This point is important when you are paid by means of a documentary letter of credit, as we shall see in Chapter 8. But remember you cannot have a dirty bill changed in any way once it has been issued.

Second, the bill of lading acts as a contract of carriage between you and the shipping line, which agrees to carry your goods to the stated destination subject to its own *conditions of carriage*. These are set out in full on the reverse of the bill, but on a short form bill they are omitted. These conditions are formidable, but as most shipments arrive safely and in good condition, it is not worth bothering about them at this stage, except to remember that if the ship cannot safely enter the designated harbour it may proceed elsewhere to off-load the goods, and it is your responsibility to see that the goods are sent on to their destination. But in practice, most shipping lines take every possible care to see that the goods do reach their final destinations. You will notice that the bill will admit that the goods are on the ship, which makes it a 'shipped bill', and is what you will require.

Third, the bill of lading acts as a title to the goods, although this is not the case with a *liner* or *sea waybill*, which you may come across. The point about the bill being a document of title is that delivery of the goods will only be made to the person holding an original bill, so that by withholding this, you can prevent delivery taking place, a point which will be discussed in Chapter 8. Hence, you must either send your customer the bill if you wish him to have the goods, or withhold it and only let him have it if, for instance, he pays or agrees to pay for the goods. In the latter case you make out the bill, not to your customer, but 'to order', and having been endorsed, it can then be passed on as you wish, or even as the customer wishes, since he might have sold the goods to someone else in the meantime.

There is a great deal more to bills of lading than this, but as a small business with comparatively few exports, these are the essentials you must know. Remember bills of lading come in sets, so many originals and so many copies, and you must decide how many of each you need when you make them out, or have them made out by the shipping line.

A *through bill* is merely one which indicates that more than one shipping line is transporting the goods, and it is issued by the first carrier. A *stale bill* is one which arrives after the goods. And a *groupage* or *house bill* is one issued by a forwarder to you for your goods, as a receipt, while he retains the original bill to enable him to clear the whole shipment.

By air
Here you are on easier ground because the airline will make out the *air waybill*, and send you your copy, the other main copies going to the consignee and the carrier. An example of an air waybill is shown in Figure 7.8 on page 110. Quite simply, it acts not as a document of title, because the goods will be delivered automatically to the consignee, but as a contract of carriage, and a receipt for the goods. Your only task will be to advise your customer by phone or telex of the number of the air

waybill so that he can get the goods on arrival. At most airports goods are stored according to their air waybill numbers.

By road and rail

Here again the documents used, a CMR (Convention de Merchandises per Routes) and a CIM (Convention Internationale de Merchandises), are made out by the carriers and act as receipts for the goods and contracts of carriage, but not as documents of title, because the goods will be delivered to the customers on arrival.

Parcel post

The Post Office will give you a receipt for the goods when you post them, and this acts as a contract of carriage between you and the Post Office. Again, delivery will be made direct to the customer, so that this document is not a document of title, although you may withhold delivery by asking the local postal services to collect the payment before delivering the goods.

Transport documents are, therefore, not in themselves difficult to make out or handle, apart from the bill of lading, especially where this is being used in conjunction with payment for the goods. We shall pick that up in the next chapter, but you can no doubt see at once the advantage you can gain by being able to decide when your customer obtains delivery according to your handling of the bill of lading.

Customs practice

Customs authorities all over the world control both the imports and exports of their countries, so there is an equivalent of HM Customs and Excise virtually everywhere. As an exporter you will be involved with Customs in two main areas, namely when your goods leave your country, and when they arrive in their country of destination, since you must ensure that your customer imports under the best possible conditions.

Customs authorities have three main tasks. First, they control the flow of both imports and exports in and out of the country. Second, they raise revenue by charging duties on imports and, occasionally, on exports. Third, they record the movement of goods coming into and leaving a country, thereby enabling the government to know its balance of trade with the rest of the world.

From Britain exports are freely permitted, except for certain specialised goods which require an *export licence*. Such goods include drugs, war materials, some chemicals, atomic energy materials and items such as antiques which are deemed to be of national value. For such goods an export licence must be obtained from the Export Licensing Branch of the Department of Trade and Industry, and it must accompany the goods so that Customs will allow them to leave the country. In addition, the Home Office has controls on dangerous drugs, while the export of live animals is controlled by the Ministry of Agriculture and Fisheries.

There are also, from time to time, restrictions placed on certain countries to which some or all goods may be exported. At present, for example, there are restrictions on what may be sent to Iran and Iraq, as well as to Vietnam. Details are to be found in Croner's *Reference Book for Exporters*.

Imports are not permitted legally into Britain without an *import licence* issued by the Department of Trade and Industry, by reason of the Import of Goods (Control) Act of 1954. This does not apply to samples, personal effects, household goods or goods for repair which will be re-exported. In practice, however, most goods are imported under an *open general licence*, except for certain goods — similar in nature to those for which export is restricted — for which a licence must be obtained. Details are given in Croner's *Reference Book for Importers*. All goods entering the UK will normally pay both import duty and VAT, in the same way that goods imported from the UK into other countries have to pay import duty and/or VAT, or its equivalent. This does not apply to the European Community or countries associated with it, since all customs duties (but not of course VAT) are progressively being abolished between member states of the Community.

To enable the correct rates of duty to be applied goods must be correctly classified. As from 1 January 1988, the classification known as the Customs Co-operation Council Nomenclature (CCCN), often referred to as the Brussels Tariff, has been superseded by the new Harmonised Commodity and Coding System (HS). This project was called Customs 88. The HS is similar to, but on a much more comprehensive scale than, the CCCN and, moreover, will be used by many more countries than the previous tariff. This is the classification you must use when describing your goods going to countries outside the EC, and also when you declare your exports to HM Customs. But, for goods going to the Community, you must use a variation of the new Harmonised System known as TARIC. This is a more detailed classification of goods and has other uses, although basically both HS and TARIC are the same.

The second change that Customs 88 made was to the procedure regarding goods going to other EC countries from Britain, or to countries associated with the Community, which are mainly EFTA countries, and certain countries around the Mediterranean. Instead of the T and EUR forms, the eight part *Single Administrative Document* (SAD) must now be used (see Figure 7.9 on page 111). This, therefore, acts as a *community movement certificate*, as well as providing evidence that the goods are in 'free circulation'. It means that the goods will not normally pay any customs duties, the aim being that this will apply to all goods by 1992. The definition of 'free circulation' is basically that the goods originated in a member state and were made of materials which have either come from the Community, or have paid the common customs tariff on being imported from outside the Community.

Third, Customs 88 has altered the procedures for declaring goods to Customs on being exported which is obligatory for all exporters, and which enables Customs to produce the figures on which the country's balance of trade is based. First, all goods should be declared to Customs before they are shipped. This is called *pre-entry* and is obligatory for all goods requiring an export licence, as well as for goods exported under CAP (Common Agricultural Policy). All these declarations must now be made on the new document (SAD).

Second, a regular exporter may, with the permission of Customs, operate a pre-shipment system, known as the *simplified clearance procedure* (SCP). In this case he is given a customs registered number (CRN) by Customs which provides the evidence that he will make the final declaration. A freight forwarder can also operate this system for his clients. Under this procedure, when the goods are despatched, a document known as an export consignment identifier (ECI) goes with them. This document may be a standard shipping note, a dangerous goods notice, a CMR or a CIM, or even a certified invoice, or air waybill. Up to 14 days after the goods have been shipped, the exporter or freight forwarder who has the CRN quoted on the documents, declares the goods to Customs using the new SAD, but making sure that the ECI quoted on the SAD is identical to that used earlier.

In addition to the pre-entry and SCP procedures there is a third method, the *local export control* (LEC) procedure, which means the goods can be cleared and declared at the exporter's warehouse or factory, but as a small business you may not wish to use this method. The SAD form will, of course, have to be used.

Should you use computers for stock control and accounting purposes, there is a fourth method, namely declaring goods to Customs by *period entry (exports)* or PE(E). This allows for periodic declarations to be made to Customs on computer-produced media. Each exporter will be allocated a CRN, under which the declarations will be made.

Remember, however, that when sending goods to another member state in the European Community for temporary use and return, you should still use a Community Carnet or an ATA (Admission Temporaire) Carnet, obtainable from a Chamber of Commerce, because this makes temporary exportation and importation that much easier.

The main benefits of Customs 88 are, first, that many customs forms have been abolished in favour of the new SAD. Second, the new classifications of goods, HS and TARIC, will make duty calculations easier and fairer for all. Third, the way has been opened in the European Community for a real Customs Union by 1992, allowing the completely free movement of goods.

Freight forwarders

As a new or small exporter you may feel, after reading the above, that arranging to ship your goods overseas, with all the attendant paperwork, is not for you, because you have neither the time nor the expertise to do it. In this case you would be well advised to use the services of what used to be called a shipping and forwarding agent, and is now called a freight forwarder.

The work of a freight forwarder will include advising you of any special requirements regarding the marking of your cargo, the packing of your cargo, and any customs requirements overseas in respect of documents etc. He will work out the best route for the shipment, the most economical routes, and obtain the best rates possible. In this respect, remember that even conference lines today are susceptible to bargaining. He can book the space on your behalf, and pay for it, since most freight is today payable in advance. This means you can pay him monthly for all your shipments. If necessary, he will arrange for your goods to be transported to the docks or airport, or arrange for the necessary instructions to be passed to your own transport people.

Provided you supply him with the basic information about the shipment, he can make out the standard shipping note, and the customs entries. He will probably have his own CRN (customs registered number), and can declare the goods on your behalf, which is an advantage if you only make occasional shipments and do not have a CRN of your own.

He will make out and have signed the various transport documents, including the bill of lading, and will despatch these as you request. He can also handle the Single Administrative Document (SAD), as well as the various special invoices or certificates of origin etc, as detailed in Chapter 8. He may even insure the goods on your behalf (insurance is considered in Chapter 10).

Moreover, many freight forwarders are now becoming involved in the actual carriage of goods, some having their own road services to European countries. Others have their own containers, which means you can send small consignments without difficulty this way. Many have developed systems of consolidated shipments by air, and can offer small exporters extremely competitive rates.

If you consult the British International Freight Association you can obtain details about them, so all you have to do is choose one and leave most of the transport side of your exporting to him. You will have to pay for the service, probably between 3 and 5 per cent of the total freight costs, plus out-of-pocket expenses and any additional document expenses.

On the other hand, you may feel that to use a freight forwarder is not cost effective and you could do it as well for less cost. Your own transport personnel may take the additional tasks of export shipments in their stride, and involving them helps to involve the whole company in export, which I have already suggested is what any small business should aim to do.

If anything goes wrong with the shipment, and your customer is dissatisfied with the service he gets, it is possible you will lose the customer. You may fire the freight forwarder but that will not necessarily regain your customer. In a recent survey less than half the exporters claimed they received a good service from their freight forwarders, about half saying it was 'fair' and the rest complaining it was poor to bad. In

EXPORT FOR THE SMALL BUSINESS

addition, half those interviewed said they could do the work as effectively, and for no more money, than the freight forwarder.

So it is not an easy choice. Much depends on the freight forwarder you choose. You want someone efficient who does not regard your business as too small to bother about to any great degree. Much also depends on how you treat your forwarder, and the service you give him. Many forwarders have never even met their clients, which is no way to produce an efficient service. Before deciding whether to use a freight forwarder, I suggest you look at the excellent book *Distribution for the Small Business* (Kogan Page). Also, *Exporter and Forwarder* (British International Freight Association) details the services freight forwarders can provide and also gives up-to-date information on new customs import regulations.

You will by now have dealt with several forms, some of which, such as the packing list, the standard shipping note, the dangerous goods form and the new SAD, will have gone with the goods. You will receive, if shipping by sea, the bills of lading, and these I suggest you carry forward to the next chapter, so to speak, because they will form part of the documents to be despatched separately, depending on how your customer is going to pay you.

Pre-shipment inspection

Although the idea of a seller insisting on the goods being inspected before they are shipped is not new, recently pre-shipment inspection is being demanded by customers in several developing countries. Moreover, the agency carrying out the inspection is also, in many cases, checking the prices charged for the goods, to make sure the buyer is not paying more for the goods than a buyer in another country.

It is often not easy to have the goods inspected and at the same time meet a shipment deadline, as called for in a letter of credit, for example, but you may find that you have no alternative but to comply with the buyer's insistence on pre-shipment inspection.

The checking of prices is rather more controversial, since if a price has been agreed in a contract it should stand.

It is hoped that the International Chamber of Commerce will be able to come up with an accepted code of conduct, but you may encounter pre-shipment inspection problems when shipping to countries like Nigeria or Zaire.

102

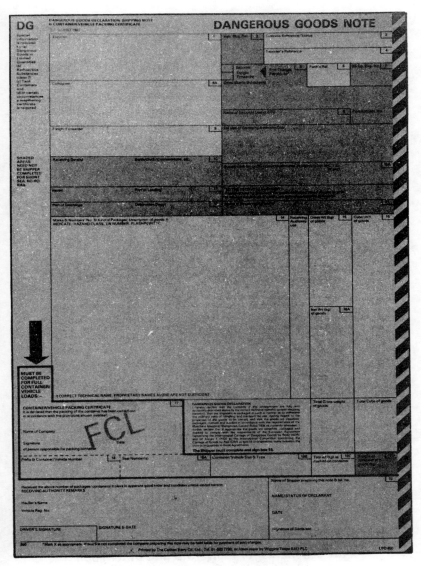

Figure 7.2 *Dangerous goods note*

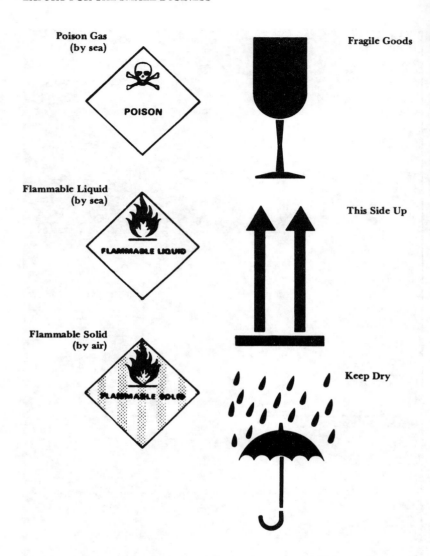

Figure 7.3 *Marks for dangerous and other goods*

```
PACKING LIST

WATSON'S GOURMET CLUB

'Charlotte'                    16 Barnhill
14 Rue de la Paix              Pinner
Nantes                         Middx
France                         Tel: 01-866 2535

                               12 August 1988


Shipped by road/ferry          Order Number P9790

W G C                          C/No. 1 - 7   120 pcs each of pork pie
Nantes                                       and steak pie
Art No. 08/358                 C/No. 8       160 pcs carawayseed cake
No. 1 - 8
W G C                          C/No. 9 -14   240 pcs stuffed marrows
Nantes
Art. No. 03/087
No. 9 - 14

W G C                          C/No. 15 -30 24 x 1 litre bottles
Nantes                                       Watson's Pickle Supreme
Art. No. 01/124
No. 15 - 30

W G C                          C/No. 31      300 packets Tartan
Nantes                                       Curry Powder
Art. No. 07/221
No. 31

W G C                          C/No. 32 -35 48 x ½ litre bottles
Nantes                                       egg and anchovy sauce
Art. No. 04/328
No. 32 - 35

TOTAL 35 cases containing 4,156 pieces

Watson's Gourmet Club



(Signature)
Manager
```

Figure 7.4 *Packing list*

SHIPPING INSTRUCTIONS				DATE 8th June 1988	

Sender

R.J. SCHULLER (UK) LIMITED
Godstone Road
Whyteleafe
Surrey CR8 1YE

Sender's ref   EXP/1/SYD

MAIL TO:

UNION TRANSPORT (LONDON) LTD
Registered Office
4-16 DEPTFORD BRIDGE
LONDON SE8 4HH
Telephone: 01-692 1234
Telex: 896021/2/3 (Unitrans London)
Telegrams: Unitrans London SE8

Consignee

SCHULER (PTY) LIMITED
P.O. Box 297
South Creek Road
Dee Why
N.S.W. 2099
Australia

Registered in England No. 417277

We will deliver to:

Your Depot in London, S.E.8

Please collect from:

N/A

For shipment per: "MORETON BAY"

Receiving/closing dates: 10.6.88

Marks/numbers	Packages	Contents	Gross	Net
ADDRESSED 1/2	1 Drum	GERANIOL "G" – NON HAZARDOUS	29 Kg	25 Kg
	1 Carton	ALDEHYDE C8 DIMETHYL ALD.	12 Kg	9 Kg
ADDRESSED 3	1 Case	MACHINERY PARTS	138 Kg	112 Kg
	N.B.	Chemicals are Non Hazardous		

Value:
£1549.00

Measurements: 1 @ 37 x 37 x 42 cms   1 @ 28 x 52 x 48 cms
1 @ 186 x 233 x 188 cms

Insurance: ☐ Cover for £   against   risks
XX Do not cover

We pay the following charges: (All other charges payable by consignee)

☐ Collection ex works
☒ FOB charges
☐ Freight to arrival
☐ Delivery to domicile

☐ Foreign customs clearance/duties
☐ Transport insurance
☐ Consular documents/cert. of origin
☐

Documentary requirements and special instructions:

We require 3 orig/ 6 copies Bill of Lading, in the name of   R.J. SCHULER (UK) LIMITED

unto consignee/order   marked Notify Consignee as above

Customs pre-entry required
No/yes (draw back papers encl)   NO

Please collect COD £

Enclosures:

☒ Commercial invoices
☒ Packing list
☐
☐
☐

Signature

13

Figure 7.5(a) *Shipping instructions*

Approved by The Institute of Freight Forwarders Ltd

© SITPRO 1982

EXPORT CARGO SHIPPING INSTRUCTIONS

Exporter/Shipper Ⓐ

For Forwarder's Use

Customs Reference/Status

Exporter's Reference

Forwarder's Ref

S S Co Bkg No

Consignee *If 'Order', state Notify Party and Address* Ⓑ

Other Address

Ⓓ

To ➡ Freight Forwarder Ⓒ

If required, this space may be used for other addresses, e g Buyer, Place of Acceptance/Delivery, additional Notify Party

Country of Origin of Goods

Country of Final Destination

Receiving/Collection Date(s)

Berth/Dock/Container base etc

If required, this space may be used for extra addresses or other information Ⓔ

Despatched By

Place of Receipt

Vessel/Aircraft etc

Port of Loading

Port of Discharge

Place of Delivery

Please insure against all risks plus war for

N B Insurance will not be effected unless instructed in writing

Marks and Numbers, No and Kind of Packages, Description of Goods*

Tariff/Trade Code No

Gross Weight (kg)

Cube (m³)

Quantity 2 for U K Customs

Net Weight

FOB Value for U K Customs (£)

Quantity 3 for U K Customs

DANGEROUS GOODS

Indicate the Correct Technical Name Hazard Class, UN Number, Flashpoint °C. and attach top copy of SITPRO Dangerous Goods Note.

Special Stowage

FREIGHT ➡

⬅ DOCUMENTATION

Inland carriage to — Groupage depot ICD / UK port/airport

Invoice Price

Certificate of Shipment

Air, Sea or other Waybill

Bill of Lading

UK Customs formalities

Consular formalities

T Forms where appropriate

Other FOB Service charges

Indicate services required, and to whom charges should be debited, by entering

Ⓐ Ⓑ Ⓒ Ⓓ or Ⓔ

in check box

Depot/ICD or port charges in U K

Freight to

Depot/ICD or port charges at destination

Oncarriage at Destination to — Depot/ICD / Place of delivery

Special Instructions

The goods ARE / ARE NOT European Community Goods

Ocean Freight Payable at

Name of Contact and Telephone Number

Make out documents as indicated and dispose of as follows

No of Bills of Lading Required

Original Copy

I We hereby declare that the above particulars are correct and agree to your published Regulations and Conditions including those as to liability

Date

Signature

340

SITPRO OVERLAYS 1982

Figure 7.5(b) *Export cargo shipping instructions (SITPRO)*

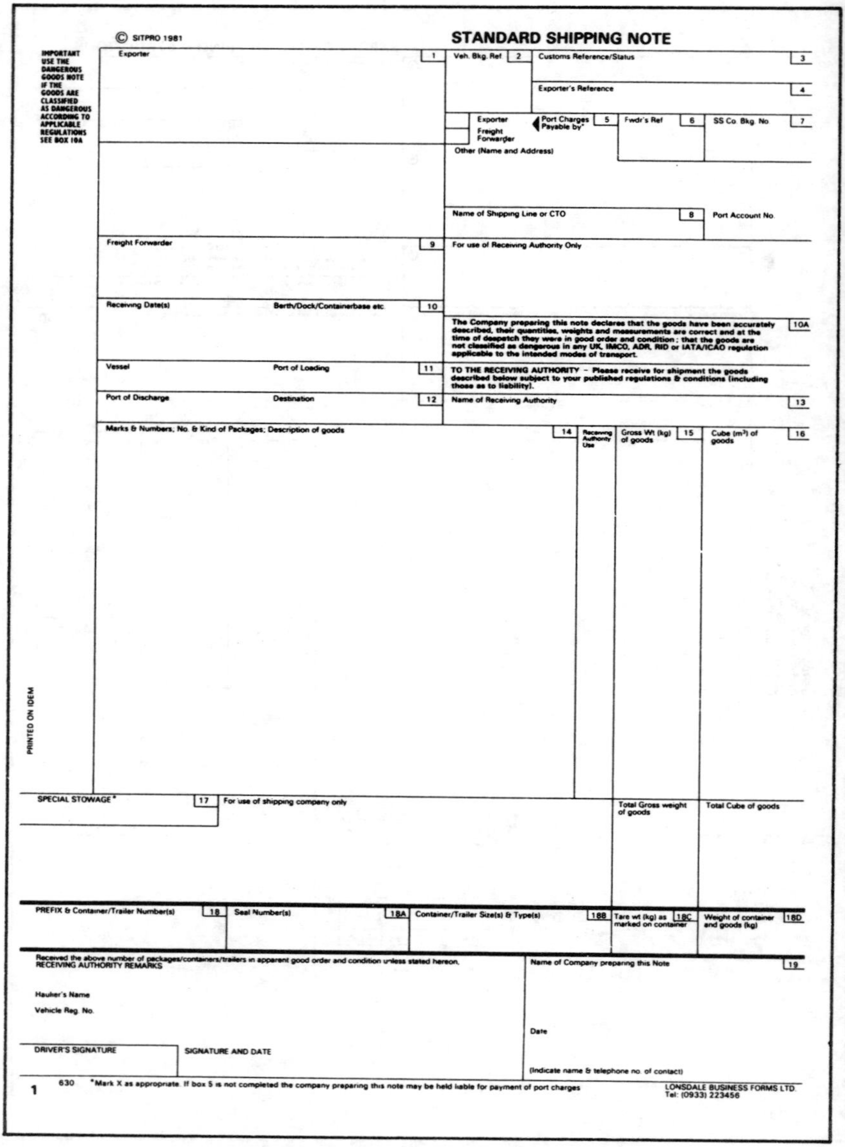

© SITPRO 1981

STANDARD SHIPPING NOTE

IMPORTANT USE THE DANGEROUS GOODS NOTE IF THE GOODS ARE CLASSIFIED AS DANGEROUS ACCORDING TO APPLICABLE REGULATIONS SEE BOX 10A

Exporter 1

Veh. Bkg. Ref. 2

Customs Reference/Status 3

Exporter's Reference 4

Exporter

Freight Forwarder

Other (Name and Address)

Port Charges Payable by* 5

Fwdr's Ref 6

SS Co. Bkg. No 7

Name of Shipping Line or CTO 8

Port Account No.

Freight Forwarder 9

For use of Receiving Authority Only

Receiving Date(s)

Berth/Dock/Containerbase etc. 10

The Company preparing this note declares that the goods have been accurately described, their quantities, weights and measurements are correct and at the time of despatch they were in good order and condition; that the goods are not classified as dangerous in any UK, IMCO, ADR, RID or IATA/ICAO regulation applicable to the intended modes of transport. 10A

Vessel

Port of Loading 11

TO THE RECEIVING AUTHORITY – Please receive for shipment the goods described below subject to your published regulations & conditions (including those as to liability).

Port of Discharge

Destination 12

Name of Receiving Authority 13

Marks & Numbers; No. & Kind of Packages; Description of goods 14

Receiving Authority Use

Gross Wt (kg) of goods 15

Cube (m³) of goods 16

PRINTED ON IDEM

SPECIAL STOWAGE* 17

For use of shipping company only

Total Gross weight of goods

Total Cube of goods

PREFIX & Container/Trailer Number(s) 18

Seal Number(s) 18A

Container/Trailer Size(s) & Type(s) 18B

Tare wt (kg) as marked on container 18C

Weight of container and goods (kg) 18D

Received the above number of packages/containers/trailers in apparent good order and condition unless stated hereon.

RECEIVING AUTHORITY REMARKS

Haulier's Name

Vehicle Reg. No.

DRIVER'S SIGNATURE

SIGNATURE AND DATE

Name of Company preparing this Note 19

Date

(Indicate name & telephone no. of contact)

1 630 *Mark X as appropriate. If box 5 is not completed the company preparing this note may be held liable for payment of port charges

LONSDALE BUSINESS FORMS LTD. Tel: (0933) 223456

Figure 7.6 *Standard shipping note*

SPECIMEN BILL OF LADING (Clients' names are fictitious)

Shipper ② QUALITY WOOLLENS LIMITED FARTHING LANE KEIGHLEY WEST YORKSHIRE	B/L No. 529 Shippers Ref. SW/4629 F/Agents Ref. S/291 ①
Consignee (If 'Order' state Notify Party) ORDER ③	**Atlantic Shipping Co** ≋
Notify Party ④ HARPER-SIMON INCORPORATED FIFTH AVENUE NEW YORK USA	Water Street Liverpool L47 2XX Tel: 051-626848 Telegraphs: Atlanco Liverpool Telex: 9978381

*Local Vessel	*From (Local Port of Loading)		
Ocean Vessel CONCORDIA ⑤	Port of Loading LIVERPOOL ⑥		
Port of Discharge NEW YORK ⑥	*Final Destination	Freight payable at BRADFORD ⑦	Number of original Bs/L THREE ⑧

Marks and Numbers	Numbers and kind of packages: Description of goods	Gross Weight KILOS	Measurement M³
QW ⑨ H-S INC. NEW YORK 1 TO 10	⑩ 10 CARTONS SHEEPSKIN COATS ⑦ FREIGHT PAID	127	0.510 cubic metres per carton

SHIPPED on board in apparent good order and condition the within mentioned Merchandise stated to be marked, numbered and described in this Bill of Lading (weight, measure, brand, contents, quality and value unknown) to be conveyed via any port or ports (for loading or discharging or for any other purpose), and as otherwise provided herein. In accepting this Bill of Lading the Shipper, Consignee, owner of the goods and the holder of the Bill of Lading expressly agree to all its terms, conditions and exceptions, whether written, printed, stamped or incorporated. Weight as shown in this Bill of Lading as declared by Shippers and the Master is unable to check same.

Number of Packages (in words) ⑪	A C Drake. ⑫	
TEN	Dated in Liverpool	1st August, 1987 ⑬

BILL OF LADING

A bill of lading is a receipt given by the shipping company upon shipment of the goods. It is a document of title and as such is required by the importer to clear the goods at the point of destination.

A bill of lading normally embodies the following details (numbers correspond to those in the example)
1. The name of the shipping company
2. The name of the exporter (shipper)
3. The name and address of the importer (consignee) or ORDER
4. The name and address of the notify party (the person to be notified on arrival of the shipment, usually the importer). This only applies when the bill has been made out to ORDER
5. The name of the carrying vessel
6. The names of the ports of shipment and discharge
7. Where freight is payable and whether it has been paid
8. The number of originals in the set
9. The marks and numbers identifying the goods
10. A brief description of the goods (possibly including weights and dimensions)
11. The number of packages
12. The signature of the ship's master or his agent
13. The date on which the goods were received for shipment and/or loaded on the vessel (this must not be later than the shipment date indicated in the credit)

Figure 7.7 *Bill of lading*

125- -8930 9065 125-8930 9065

Shipper's Name and Address	Shippers account Number
N P A LTD c/o E HIGGS AIR AGENCY LTD 28/29 ST JOHNS LANE LONDON E C I	

Not negotiable
Air Waybill
(Air Consignment note)
Issued by
British Airways London
Member of IATA

British airways

Copies 1, 2 and 3 of this Air Waybill are originals and have the same validity

Consignee's Name and Address	Consignee's account Number
AL AHRAM ESTABLISHMENT 31 AL GALAA STREET CAIRO	

It is agreed that the goods described herein are accepted in apparent good order and condition (except as noted) for carriage SUBJECT TO THE CONDITIONS OF CONTRACT ON THE REVERSE HEREOF. THE SHIPPER'S ATTENTION IS DRAWN OF THE NOTICE CONCERNING CARRIERS' LIMITATION OF LIABILITY. Shipper may increase such limitation of liability by declaring a higher value for carriage and paying a supplemental charge if required.

Issuing Carrier's Agent Name and City
E HIGGS AIR AGENCY LTD
28/29 ST JOHNS LANE LONDON E C I

Accounting Information

Agent's IATA Code   Account No.

Airport of departure (Addr. of first Carrier) and requested Routing
LONDON

CHARGES PREPAID

to	By first Carrier	Routing and Destination	to	by	to	by	Currency	CHGS Code	WT/VAL PPD COLL	Other PPD COLL	Declared Value for Carriage	Declared Value for Customs
							UK£				NDV	82.600

Airport of Destination	Flight/Date	For Carrier Use only	Flight/Date
CAIRO			

Handling Information

CSRL83

No of Pieces RCP	Gross Weight kg lb	Rate Class Commodity Item No.	Chargeable Weight	Rate / Charge	Total	Nature and Quantity of Goods (incl. Dimensions or Volume)
9	118.k		118.k	1.320		ENGLISH NEWSPAPERS

Prepaid	Weight Charge	Collect	Other Charges
155.760			AWB FEE I 500 HANDLING 6.500

Valuation Charge

Tax

Total other Charges Due Agent
1.500

Total other Charges Due Carrier
6.500

Shipper certifies that the particulars on the face hereof are correct and that insofar as any part of the consignment contains restricted articles, such part is properly described by name and is in proper condition for carriage by air according to the International Air Transport Association's Restricted Articles Regulations.

E HIGGS AIR AGENCY LTD

Signature of Shipper or his Agent

Total prepaid	Total collect

Currency Conversion Rates	cc charges in Dest. Currency
163.760	

8.8.1983   London   Higgs. EX.

Executed on   (Date)   at   (Place)   Signature of Issuing Carrier or its Agent

For Carrier Use only at Destination	Charges at Destination	Total collect Charges

125-8930 9065

M. 197 - 1 st.
Printed in the Fed. Rep. Germany Bartsch Verlag, Munich-Ottobrunn 600 ¡ (6l)

Copy 6 - (Third Carrier)

Figure 7.8 *Air waybill*

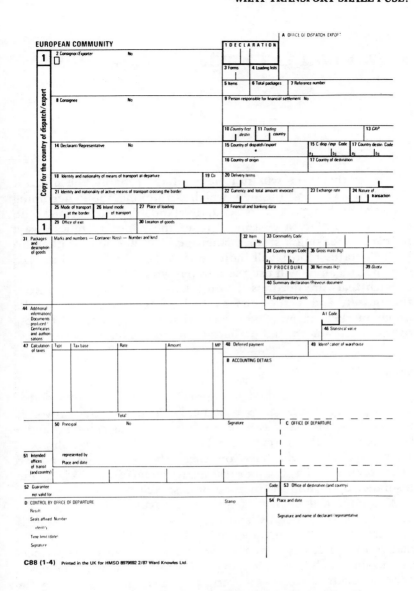

Figure 7.9 *Single Administrative Document (SAD)*

Chapter 8

How Can I Get Paid?

The fear that you will not be paid is probably the greatest worry of any small business which is thinking about becoming involved with export. It is an understandable fear because who is to say whether a customer many thousands of miles away, probably speaking a strange language, is either able or likely to pay? A status report will indicate if he has the funds, but that does not mean he will use them to pay you.

Such fears are needless if you take sensible precautions from the outset, and with so many bad debts now current in the home market, it may be argued that dealing with customers overseas is no more, and perhaps even less, risky.

Invoices

The basic document used in export is an invoice, but whereas people pay against invoices at home, in the export trade invoices are used in the main as a record of the goods shipped, and a statement of the terms on which they have been shipped. Therefore, they will have on them the marks, weights and measurements of the goods, along with details of freight and insurance costs, and the method of despatch.

A commercial invoice, as shown in Figure 8.1 on page 124, contains all these details, and will only be used for payment if you are giving your customer open account terms. Even then, in many countries, payment may not be made against the invoice, but against a Bill of Exchange or Draft. You will, however, need to send customers a certain number of copies of your commercial invoice with each shipment, the number depending on the customer's local requirements which you must always ascertain.

A *pro forma invoice* is no more than an invoice used for making quotations, and has the words 'pro forma' written on it. Where payment is made in advance, it would be used as a means of obtaining payment from the importer.

Invoices, however, are used for customs purposes when an importer receives the goods, so that they become *certificates of value and origin*. In some cases, the commercial invoice need only be signed by the exporter, and will be accepted by customs in the importer's country as a true declaration of the value and origin of the goods, on which customs duty will then be determined.

In many countries, however, invoices, along with their declarations of value and origin, must be made out on special forms, and details of such requirements will be found in Croner's *Reference Book for Exporters*. Nigeria, for example, requires the use of Form 731, while Zambia uses Form 737, and the Caribbean countries generally use Form 520. So check if the importer's country has any special requirements before you start making out the invoices. Such invoices are known as customs invoices.

In other countries the declaration of the exporter is insufficient, and here *certified invoices* will be required. Such certified invoices are in effect certificates of origin, and in Figure 8.2 on page 125 there is a specimen certificate of origin. You may need to have invoices certified by your own local Chamber of Commerce.

When shipping to Middle East countries, not only must your commercial invoices be legalised by the consulate of the country concerned, but you must also obtain a certificate of origin from the Arab-British Chamber of Commerce.

In many South American countries *consular invoices* are required. You obtain the form from the relevant embassy and have to get it signed by an embassy official after filling it in.

Remember that you will usually have to pay to have invoices or certificates of origin etc stamped by both Chambers of Commerce and embassies or consulates. Moreover, this all takes time, an important point when you must supply all the necessary documents to the bank against a letter of credit within a certain time.

Some countries insist on invoices being made out or containing a declaration in their own language, but Croner's has all these details so that the procedures are not as complicated as they may sound.

The invoice is the first document you will have to prepare, and note that your freight forwarder, if you use one, cannot do this for you, although he may be able to prepare and obtain all the other certificates of origin required. But you will have

113

already prepared all the basic information about a shipment, as detailed in the previous chapter, so making out the invoice should present no serious problems.

Invoices are, therefore, a means of knowing how much you require to be paid, as well as helping an importer to know what has been sent to him, what he has to pay, and to get the goods through his customs. What has to be considered next are the various methods by which you, as an exporter, can be paid, and then which will be the most suitable to use.

Cash in advance

From your point of view this is an ideal method of payment, because you have both the money and the goods, and you can then send the goods overseas, knowing your customer has already paid for them. From his point of view, however, it is not very satisfactory, since he has paid his money but has no guarantee that you will actually send him the goods. However, with a new and, to you, totally unknown customer you would be justified in asking for payment in advance.

Such payment would be made against a commercial or pro forma invoice, and the money could be sent to you by cheque, in which case you would need to wait until the cheque was cleared before despatching the goods, which could be some weeks. A *banker's draft* would be more satisfactory because this is a cheque issued by the bank, although such drafts are not commonly used, owing to the possibility of their being stolen. Generally, payments are made by means of a mail or telex transfer, while there is a computerised system used by banks for transferring money called SWIFT. This stands for the Society of Worldwide Interbank Financial Telecommunications, a Belgian Co-operative owned by the largest European and American banks.

You can always offer a discount for payment in advance, but beware of the customer who offers a deposit in advance with a promise to pay the balance on the arrival of the goods, because he may well not pay that balance and thus obtain the goods at a discount. Only allow this if you can make certain that he will not get the goods unless he pays the balance. This is often done when long-term contracts are involved but, as a small exporter, you are unlikely to be concerned with these.

Documentary letters of credit

This method of payment involves an importer asking his bank to open a credit in favour of an exporter. He will lay down certain conditions under which the exporter may be paid, normally that the goods must be despatched according to his instructions, and that the documents needed to obtain delivery of the goods are provided. The importer's bank will then request a bank in the exporter's country to advise the exporter of the credit, and the conditions attached to it, and provided these are carried out, to pay the exporter accordingly.

From the importer's point of view this is more satisfactory because he knows that the goods have been shipped according to his instructions, and that he will not be paying for them unless this has been done. From your point of view you know that, provided you carry out the instructions issued by the importer, you will be paid. However, this is on two assumptions. First, that the credit is *irrevocable*. This means it cannot be altered without the consent of the four parties concerned. Hence, you should normally accept only irrevocable credits, although if you know your customer well, you might accept a revocable one, because you are sure he will not revoke it. The second assumption is that it is a *confirmed* credit. This means that the money has been credited to a bank in your country, and that the money will be paid to you, whereas if the credit is unconfirmed, the credit is still in the importer's bank, and circumstances could arise whereby that credit could not be transferred to you, as when all transfers of currency between the importer's country and Britain are forbidden. Therefore, you should always accept only a confirmed credit. You can insure against non-payment of an unconfirmed letter of credit, as we shall see in Chapter 10, but you will not receive the full value of the credit, so it is better to insist on a confirmed credit. Moreover, make sure the credit is confirmed by a reputable bank, because the only time when you will not get your money is if the bank goes bust. It is true that this has happened only occasionally, but you cannot afford to take chances.

An example of a documentary letter of credit is shown in Figure 8.3 on page 126, and when you receive one you must check it carefully to make sure you can comply with all the conditions laid down. Make sure the goods you are supplying exactly match those described on the credit. Check the total amount of the credit to see that it covers all you expect to receive, because although you can be paid less, you cannot be paid one penny more, so it is wise to insist on the total being over rather than under what you expect to receive. Check, if any date of shipment is specified, that you can ship before that date, and make sure that you will be able to obtain all the documents required before the expiry date of the credit, because nothing will be paid if the credit has expired.

Leave nothing to chance. For example, if a full set of shipped on board bills of lading is specified, ask the advising bank what they mean by a full set, because opinions differ as to how many originals and how many copies comprise a full set. Check that any special conditions can be complied with; for example, if shipment has to be made by a certain shipping line or may not be made by a particular line — the Arabs do not accept shipments made by an Israeli line.

Once you are satisfied with all the terms of the credit you may accept it, but if there is anything in it with which you cannot agree, have it altered by the importer at once. And make sure that all charges are for the buyer's account.

The people you must send a copy of the credit to will be those responsible for producing, packing and shipping the goods (including your freight forwarder if you use one), as well as those responsible for preparing the documents, insuring the goods and handling the credit with the bank concerned.

Having despatched the goods and collected all the documents called for in the credit, you take these to the advising and confirming bank with a draft drawn at sight (explained later in this chapter), and you will be paid. This means you receive your money after shipment but possibly before the goods reach the importer, depending on how far away he is.

The rules and regulations for documentary letters of credit have been codified by the International Chamber of Commerce under the heading of 'Uniform Customs and Practice for Documentary Credits' (Document 290). These were revised in 1983, and came into effect in 1984. You should only accept a credit if it is so marked, and if you wish to know more about the details of credits, study these rules.

There are several other types of credit which you may come across and wish to use. For example, a *transferable credit* is one which may be transferred in whole or in part to a third party, so you could use it to pay a supplier if you wished. A *revolving credit* is one where there is continuous trade between an exporter and an importer, and to save the credit being opened each time, the one credit is automatically renewed. A *red clause credit* allows the advising bank to advance some of the money to an exporter, so called because this clause used to be written in red ink. A *back to back credit* is when an exporter himself opens a credit in favour of a supplier, using the original credit from the importer as security.

Documentary letters of credit are extensively used for payment in export, and as a small company you can accept them, secure in the knowledge that you will be paid provided you carry out the terms laid down in the credit. But note that a survey showed that some 60 per cent of credits presented to the banks contained some errors, which led to delays in payment. As a small company, you cannot afford any delay in payment, so make sure you do not join the ranks of the 60 per cent by presenting incorrect documents to the advising or confirming bank and then expecting to be paid.

Bills of exchange

From a customer's point of view, opening a credit in favour of an exporter means he has to tie up his money and, in many cases, pay before he receives the goods. He may therefore prefer to pay after he has taken delivery. From the exporter's point of view, he may wish to allow credit to his customers overseas, but at the same time will want to ensure that he will be paid. A bill of exchange will enable him to do this, especially if he is shipping the goods by sea, and can use the bill of lading to withhold delivery in the event of non-payment by the importer.

Although the document used is a bill of exchange, it is customary to refer to it, in its initial stages, as a *draft*, which is drawn on a customer by the exporter. The procedure is thus the opposite to that of a documentary letter of credit, because the exporter draws the draft on a customer, and sends it to his bank with instructions to forward it to a correspondent bank in the importer's country. This bank presents the draft to the importer, and if he pays the draft, or agrees to pay it at a later date, he is then handed the documents enabling him to take delivery of the goods. Even if shipment is not by sea, a draft can still be drawn on a customer, because it is a legal document demanding payment, and if this is refused the drawer has legal backing to obtain the money.

Drafts are of two kinds. The first is a *sight draft* (see Figure

117

8.4 on page 127), which means that it is payable at sight by the person on whom it is drawn. When the bank in the importer's country receives the sight draft, it presents the draft to the importer and, provided he pays it, the documents enabling delivery to take place are handed to him.

Second, there are *term drafts*, which are payable at so many days, calculated in multiples of 30 days, after sight. The procedure is for the local bank to present this term draft to the importer, and if he agrees to pay it on the due date, he writes 'Accepted' on it, when he is given the documents to enable him to take delivery of the goods. The bank will then return this accepted draft (which can now properly be termed a bill of exchange) to the exporter's bank, who will give it to the exporter. He can either retain it until it is paid by the importer, or discount it for cash (see Chapter 9). The proceeds of a sight draft are, of course, remitted to the exporter in accordance with his instructions.

You will notice the protection given to the exporter in that his goods are not handed over in the case of a sight draft unless the importer pays. But in the case of a term draft the importer gets the goods, and may not pay the exporter on the due date. To this extent the exporter is at risk, so you should not grant importers credit in this way unless you know them and are reasonably sure they will pay. In addition, you will also run the risk that moneys paid by an importer against drafts cannot be remitted to you, because of some action which prevents the transfer of currency from the importer's country to Britain. But as you will see in Chapter 10, you can insure against this happening, although not quite to the full amount.

When you draw a draft on an importer in this way you send it to your bank with instructions as to what you wish them to do with it, on a *bills for collection form*, as shown in Figure 8.5 on page 128. These instructions are quite precise, especially regarding what the local bank is to do in case of non-payment or non-acceptance. Is, for example, the draft to be protested; that is, should the bank inform everyone that the importer has not met his liabilities, which means his credit rating is destroyed? Are the goods to be returned to the exporter, or sold to another customer if one can be found? How is the money to be remitted and so on? But that is for you to decide. You will also indicate clearly the documents you are providing to be transmitted overseas.

The procedure and responsibilities for drafts have been

codified by the International Chamber of Commerce and set down in the 'Uniform Rules for the Collection of Commercial Paper', and these explain in great detail what takes place, what the banks do etc. Further information about bills of exchange and documentary credits is to be found in *Raising Finance*, a *Guardian* guide for small businesses.

If you now refer back to documentary letters of credit, you will remember that to obtain your money from the advising and confirming bank, you have to draw a draft payable at sight for the total amount you are claiming against the credit on the bank. This is done because you are then making a legal request to the bank to pay you, which is what the banks will usually ask you for.

If you come across the terms *documents against payment* (DP) and *documents against acceptance* (DA), these are merely used for requesting payment against a sight draft, or a term draft. The term CAD, or *cash against documents*, is also used instead of DP.

Open account

When you know a customer overseas very well, you may wish to allow him to pay you on open account, and you will probably have laid it down in your conditions of sale what you expect in this respect. For example, you may state that you expect payment in the month following the receipt of the goods.

In this case all the documents can go directly to the importer to enable him to take delivery, and you rely on him to pay on the due date. You may insure against his inability to pay (see Chapter 10), but clearly this is of the greatest value to a customer, while from your point of view it gives little protection, and is to be used with some caution.

However, in many countries payment will not be made against an invoice, and you may be asked to draw a draft for the amount, payable on the due date, such a draft not being used in connection with the documents. France, for example, always pays this way, as a French customer seldom pays against an invoice. It is a highly satisfactory way of dealing with open account, since no customer should object to a draft if he has every intention of paying you on the due date.

These are the four main ways of getting paid for your exports, and it is up to you to decide which you wish to use in each case. On the other hand, you may feel that you do not wish to be involved with getting money from customers, but would prefer to subcontract the work to an outside company.

Factoring

For a small business, factoring may well be of interest, because it is a way of leaving the collection of money from customers to a factoring company, who will be totally responsible for collecting the money and paying you. In most cases factors are controlled by the banks, and there is an Association of British Factors, whose members will be prepared to work for you.

All you do in effect is to hand over the export sales accounting function to a factor, who not only checks the importer's credit standing, but also collects the money, generally guaranteeing 100 per cent payment to the exporter, whether or not the importer has paid. Factoring thus saves the exporter a great deal of clerical work. It eliminates any foreign exchange risks. It also enables an exporter to deal with an importer on open account terms without the fear that the importer will not pay.

For this service an exporter will have to pay somewhere between 2½ and 3½ per cent, which may well be less than it would cost him to set up an export accounting system.

The main development in factoring is that factoring companies are starting to operate in pairs, one company in Britain working with other companies overseas. The factor in Britain looks after the exporter's sales ledger, while the overseas factor checks the customers' credit, collects the money, and takes the risk if payment is not made. Another development is that factoring companies are providing shipping and forwarding services to exporters, which means you can subcontract both your shipping and your payment work and problems to a factor.

In addition, a factoring company will pay an exporter up to about 75 per cent of the value of payments outstanding, as soon as they are advised of such amounts. For this the factor will charge around 3 per cent above base rate, so it is a relatively expensive way for an exporter to obtain cash and you should not consider a factor's services basically as a means of obtaining money.

For a small businessman involved with export, factoring has obvious attractions, not least because he should always have a clear knowledge of the state of his accounts overseas, both new and old; even regular and well paying customers can get into severe financial difficulties. Many exporters have found to their cost that their most reliable overseas customers have lost them the most money. Certainly with so much export business being done in Europe and the United States on open account, any exporter must consider factoring seriously.

Forfaiting

If you are an exporter of capital goods and are required to give long-term credit overseas, you should be aware of the system known as forfaiting. This is operated by a number of City firms and, in brief, what happens is that you, as the exporter, sell the total amount you are owed for the whole contract to the forfaiter for a discount. You are then paid that amount, so you have no further worries that the importer might not pay the full amount of the contract. The importer must have a reputable local bank to guarantee payment, but the forfaiter collects the money over the length of the credit. Hence, forfaiting is something similar to factoring, but on a larger scale, so it is beyond the resources of most factors. It is being used a good deal with contracts for capital goods in South America, Eastern Europe and some countries in the Far East, where the political risk of non-payment is high. This area of payment will be covered in Chapter 10, because there is an alternative to forfaiting, but it is worth remembering should you become involved with supplying capital goods where long-term credit is demanded.

Countertrade

Because so many countries suffer from a lack of foreign exchange with which to pay for their imports, paying with goods instead of money is becoming increasingly popular. So when a customer overseas is unable to pay, you may offer him the alternative of paying in kind rather than money.

There are several kinds of countertrade, one being *barter*. This is a straightforward exchange of goods, made without any money changing hands or any intermediaries being used. It is fairly rare today.

Counterpurchase is more common: an exporter is asked to buy goods from the importer in exchange for goods he has supplied, such goods representing some or all of the total value of the export consignment.

Compensation/Buyback is where the technical know-how,

121

and perhaps some equipment, is supplied by an exporter, who guarantees to buy back the finished product up to the total amount involved in supplying the technology etc.

Finally, *switch trading* is where an exporter is paid by someone in a third country.

You are unlikely to become involved with these, apart from *counterpurchase*, but you should be prepared to handle this since it can be profitable. Unless the goods on offer are raw materials you would need to buy, you are unlikely to want them. In this case, your procedure should be, first, to contact a factor who will arrange the sale of the goods you agree to take from the importer. (There are many such factors, some in the City and others in Vienna, Berlin and so on.) The factors will give you a price they will receive for the goods, less their commission, which is usually of the order of 15 to 20 per cent. Using this price, you can then quote your products to the importer in terms of such goods; for example, you will sell one accounting machine for three cases of vodka. Your goods are then shipped to the buyer according to the factor's instructions, who pays you when he receives payment from the buyer. It may sound both involved and risky, but having been involved in several such transactions myself, I can assure you that if you use a good factor, it all works highly satisfactorily.

Foreign currencies

You will have noticed that throughout this chapter I have suggested that payment will be made to you from overseas in your own currency, namely sterling. This assumes of course that you have quoted your customer in sterling, although in Chapter 4 I suggested that it might be more beneficial to a customer to be quoted in his own currency. As you will appreciate, a buyer always pays in his own currency, because that is all he has. A seller in the end always receives payment in his own currency because that is all he can use. In these days of floating exchange rates, a seller, if he quotes in his customer's currency, will take the risk that when that currency is turned into sterling, the exchange rate may differ from that current at the time the contract was made. In the same way, a buyer agreeing to a sterling price does not know for sure what he will have to pay in his own currency for that sterling, since the rate may have changed since he ordered the goods and has to pay for them.

Clearly, therefore, if you quote an importer in his own currency, you are taking the risk of fluctuation in the exchange rate between that currency and sterling. While you may gain, you may equally well lose. A similar state of affairs would exist if you were buying from another country and had to pay in sterling for the currency with which to pay your supplier. You might pay more or you might pay less.

Variations in rates of exchange between sterling and the currencies in your customers' countries are of importance to you, and you will need to keep a running check on them, however you quote, because variations affect the prices at which you offer to sell, and therefore, your competitiveness.

At the same time, unless you are paid in advance, or by a confirmed irrevocable letter of credit, you run the risk of not having the currency with which your customer pays you exchanged for sterling, because there is no free exchange of the two currencies. How you can insure against this risk will be dealt with in Chapter 10, but in the next chapter we will examine how you can eliminate exchange risks, so that a customer can be safely quoted in his own currency. At the same time we will consider which of the methods of payment you might profitably use, and why, because the choice may make all the difference between a profit or loss on export.

In the meantime, before looking at ways by which you can ensure a reasonable contribution to revenue from your exports, you should consult your bank and have their views on how best you can ask to be paid, as well as how they can help you with your cash flow etc. Unless you opt for factoring, you are going to use your bank's services to a major degree, and they offer so many services that you should be familiar with them. You should also be on good terms with your bank if you want them to process your documents and so on. As a small company you will probably have a rather better chance of success and certainly more banking facilities than a large company, because the banks are as anxious as anyone to improve the amount of exporting done by small firms. So if you are still seriously thinking of tackling export, now is the time to discuss payment and other matters with your bank.

SPECIMEN INVOICE (Clients' names are fictitious)

① # QUALITY WOOLLENS LTD.

PO BOX 71, FARTHING LANE, KEIGHLEY, WEST YORKSHIRE BD1 9X
Telephone Keighley (0535) 9461

② Harper-Simon Incorporated
Fifth Avenue
New York
U.S.A.

③ Date 11th August, 1987

Invoice No. 124

QUANTITY	DESCRIPTION		AMOUNT	
100	Ladies Sheepskin Coats ④ 25 each of Models: Moorland, Dalesman, Fells and Wensleydale			
	Ex-works price £80 each ⑤ All freight charges and export packing Insurance from warehouse to warehouse		£8000 210 30	00 00 00
	⑥ C.I.F. New York	⑦ Total	£8240	00
Marks & Nos.	⑧ ⑨ Packed in 10 cardboard cartons – 10 per carton			
QW ⑪ H-S INC. NEW YORK 1-10	⑩ Import Licence No. LHDL 22 1987			
	per pro Quality Woollens Ltd.			
	⑫ Joe Arkwright			

INVOICE

An invoice gives details of the goods which are the basis of the transaction between the exporter and the importer. It is usually completed on the exporter's own headed invoice form, and several copies are normally required for use by Customs and Excise authorities overseas.

The invoice must carry a description of the goods, stating prices and terms exactly as specified in the credit, as well as shipping marks. The following details are usually required and the inclusion of other information may be necessary (numbers correspond to those in the example)

1. Exporter's name and address
2. Importer's name and address
3. Place and date of issue
4. Description of the goods
5. Cost of freight and insurance (if specifically requested)
6. Shipment terms
7. Total amount payable
8. Number and type of packages
9. The contents of individual packages
10. The export and/or import licence numbers
11. Marks and numbers on packages
12. Signature of the exporter.

Figure 8.1 *Commercial invoice*

	Packages			Weight	

Consignor:
Quality Woollens Limited
Farthing Lane
Keighley
West Yorks

B 629546

Consignee:
Harper-Simon Limited
Fifth Avenue
New York, USA

CERTIFICATE OF ORIGIN

Consignment by:
Ship – CONCORDIA

THE BRADFORD CHAMBER OF
COMMERCE AND INDUSTRY

THE UNDERSIGNED AUTHORITY certifies that the goods shown below

Serial No.	Packages Number and kind	Packages Marks and numbers	Description of goods	Weight gross	Weight net
	10 cartons	QW H-S INC NEW YORK 1-10	Sheepskin Coats	127KS	

CHAMBER OF COMMERCE
3 AUG 1987
CERTIFYING STAMP

Originated in:

European Communities – United Kingdom

B. Caharine.

Bradford, 3rd August 1987
Place and date of issue

The Bradford Chamber of Commerce and Industry
(Name, signature and stamp of competent Authority)

CERTIFICATE OF ORIGIN

This is a signed declaration stating the country of origin of the goods. It is required by the customs authority of certain countries for the purposes of assessing import duty. Generally it has to be authenticated by a UK chamber of commerce.

Figure 8.2 *Certificate of origin*

SPECIMEN DOCUMENTARY CREDIT (Clients' names are fictitious)

BRITISH NATIONAL

Pennine House, 45 Well Street, Bradford, W. Yorks

Date   20th July, 1987
① IRREVOCABLE CREDIT No.   FDC/2/6789
To be quoted on all drafts and correspondence.

Beneficiary(ies)   ②
Quality Woollens Limited
Farthing Lane, Keighley,
West Yorks.

Advised through

Accreditor   ③
Harper-Simon Incorporated,
Fifth Avenue,
New York, U.S.A.

To be completed only if applicable

Our cable of

Advised through   refers

Dear Sir(s),
In accordance with instructions received from   The State Banking Co.
we hereby issue in your favour a Documentary Credit for   £8240
(say)   Eight thousand, two hundred and forty pounds sterling   ④   available by
your drafts drawn on   us
at sight
for the   100% c.i.f.⑥   invoice value, accompanied by the following documents:

1. Invoice in triplicate, signed and marked Licence No.
   LHDL 22 1987
⑦ 2. Certificate of origin issued by a Chamber of Commerce
3. Full set of clean on board Shipping Company's Bills of Lading made out
   to order and blank endorsed, marked "Freight Paid" and
   "Notify Harper-Simon Inc. Fifth Avenue, New York"
4. Insurance Policy or Certificate in duplicate, covering Marine and
   War Risks up to buyer's warehouse, for invoice value of the goods.

Covering the following goods:
⑧   100 Sheepskin Coats
⑨ To be shipped from   Liverpool   to   New York c.i.f.   ⑥
not later than   10th August, 1987
⑩ Partshipment   not permitted   Transhipment   not permitted
This credit is available for   presentation to us   until   31st August, 1987   ⑪
Documents to be presented within 21 days of shipment but within
credit validity
Drafts drawn hereunder must be marked "Drawn under British National Bank,
Pennine House, 45 Well Street, Bradford   branch,
Credit number   FDC/2/6789
⑫ We undertake that drafts and documents drawn under and in strict conformity with
the terms of this credit will be honoured upon presentation.

Yours faithfully,

Co-signed (Signature No.   )   Signed (Signature No.   )

DOCUMENTARY CREDIT

This is a typical irrevocable letter of credit — most credits are fairly similar in appearance and contain the following details (numbers correspond to those in the example):

1. The type of credit (revocable or irrevocable)
2. The name and address of the exporter (beneficiary)
3. The name and address of the importer (accreditor)
4. The amount of the credit in sterling or a foreign currency
5. The name of the party on whom the bills of exchange are to be drawn, and whether they are to be at sight or of a particular tenor
6. the terms of contract and shipment (i.e. whether ex-works, FOB, CIF, etc.)
7. Precise instructions as to the documents against which payment is to be made
8. A brief description of the goods covered by the credit
9. Shipping details, including whether transhipments are allowed. Also recorded is the latest date for shipment and the names of the ports of shipment and discharge
10. Whether the credit is available for one or several shipments
11. The expiry date
12. Credit confirmed by bank in beneficiary's country — adds *certainty* to payment.

Figure 8.3 *Documentary letter of credit*

SPECIMEN BILL OF EXCHANGE (Clients' names are fictitious)

⑧
£8,240

Keighley
11th August, 1987

⑦ ① ⑥ ⑨
AT SIGHT OF THIS SOLA OF EXCHANGE PAY TO OUR ORDER THE SUM OF STERLING

POUNDS EIGHT THOUSAND TWO HUNDRED AND FORTY ONLY FOR VALUE RECEIVED

Drawn under Irrevocable Credit of British National Bank, Pennine House, 45 Well Street,

Bradford No. FDC/2/6789 dated 20th July 1987

③ ⑤
To: British National Bank
         Pennine House
         45 Well Street
         Bradford

②
For and on behalf of
QUALITY WOOLLENS LTD
④

Director

The legal definition of a bill of exchange is:

1. an unconditional order in writing
2. addressed by one person (the drawer)
3. to another (the drawee)
4. signed by the person giving it (the drawer)
5. requiring the person to whom it is addressed (the drawee, who when he signs becomes the acceptor)
6. to pay
7. on demand or at a fixed or determinable future time
8. a sum certain in money
9. to, or to the order of, a specified person or to bearer (the payee).

The phrases are numbered to correspond to the various parts of the bill of exchange shown above. All the information above must be shown on every bill of exchange.

The specimen bill of exchange is a 'sight' bill which requires immediate payment by the drawee. If it called for payment after the date of the bill it would be a 'tenor' bill. Unless the documentary letter of credit stipulates that bills of exchange are required in duplicate, a single (sola) bill of exchange is acceptable.

Figure 8.4 *Sight draft*

CLEAN OR DOCUMENTARY FOREIGN BILLS FOR ACCEPTANCE OR COLLECTION OR NEGOTIATION.

BRANCH COLLECTION NUMBER

BRANCH CODE NUMBER   DATE

The choice of a correspondent rests with Lloyds Bank unless instructions are given on this form to present through a named bank direct without the intervention of any intermediary.

Airmail is used wherever possible unless otherwise instructed. Duplicate documents are normally sent by surface mail.

PLEASE FOLLOW INSTRUCTIONS WHICH I/WE HAVE MARKED ⊠ BELOW.

I WE ENCLOSE

| FOR COLLECTION | | FOR ACCEPTANCE AND RETURN |
| FOR ACCEPTANCE AND COLLECTION | | FOR NEGOTIATION |

BILL OF EXCHANGE (*Insert sole, first, second, etc.*)   AMOUNT _____

TENOR   CLAUSED AS FOLLOWS:

DRAWERS' NAME AND TOWN

Signed copies of bills of lading should be denoted thus 1 1 2 3 etc. Unsigned copies should be recorded separately.

DOCUMENTS	STATE-MENT	INVOICES		CERT OF ORIGIN	SPECIFIC-ATION	POLICY OR CERT OF INS	BILL OF LADING	AIR CON. NOTE	PARCEL RECEIPT		
		COMM'L	CERT'D	CONSULAR								
NUMBER OF COPIES												

BILL OF LADING DATED _____   NAME OF VESSEL _____

AIR CONSIGNMENT NOTE } DATED _____   ADDRESSED }

PARCEL RECEIPT   ISSUED AT _____   TO }

WHEREABOUTS OF ANY MISSING BILL OF LADING

GOODS

| ⊠ **INSTRUCT YOUR CORRESPONDENTS TO RELEASE DOCUMENTS AGAINST** } → | ACCEPTANCE | |
| | PAYMENT | (*If no bill of exchange state amount*) |

PROTEST IF UNACCEPTED		PROTEST IF UNPAID
DO NOT PROTEST IF UNACCEPTED		DO NOT PROTEST IF UNPAID
RE-PRESENT ON ARRIVAL OF GOODS IF NOT HONOURED ON FIRST PRESENTATION		COLLECT ALL CHARGES
		WAIVE CHARGES IF REFUSED
ADVISE ACCEPTANCE BY CABLE GIVING DUE DATE		IF DOCUMENTS NOT TAKEN UP ON ARRIVAL OF GOODS, WAREHOUSE GOODS IF POSSIBLE
ADVISE ACCEPTANCE BY AIRMAIL GIVING DUE DATE		IF DOCUMENTS NOT TAKEN UP ON ARRIVAL OF GOODS, INSURE GOODS AGAINST FIRE
ADVISE NON-ACCEPTANCE BY CABLE GIVING REASON		: Specify other risks, if any :
ADVISE NON-ACCEPTANCE BY AIRMAIL GIVING REASON		ADVISE NON-PAYMENT BY CABLE GIVING REASON
		ADVISE NON-PAYMENT BY AIRMAIL GIVING REASON

| IN CASE OF NEED REFER TO _____ → |
| FOR INFORMATION ONLY |
| AND TAKE HIS THEIR INSTRUCTIONS WITHOUT RESERVE |
| AND TAKE HIS/THEIR INSTRUCTIONS AS TO ALTERATION OF AMOUNT OR TENOR OF BILL |

| REMIT NET PROCEEDS BY CABLE |
| REMIT NET PROCEEDS BY AIRMAIL |
| ⊠ OTHER INSTRUCTIONS |

Figure 8.5 *Bills for collection form*

Chapter 9
How Can I Make Money From Export?

Much of the emphasis in this book has been on the importance of making money from export, because without it there is little point in any small business becoming involved. You will recall that in Chapter 4 I suggested that, before arriving at any export price, you should always take into account, not only how an export customer will pay, but when he will pay. This involves your deciding which method of payment you will use from those described in the previous chapter, and to do this requires you to have a system of export credit control.

Credit control

Before an export order can be accepted it must be passed by credit control, because you are unlikely to agree to ship goods to a customer who may not pay you, owes money from a previous order, or is likely to be slow in paying. Credit control must be applied both to new customers and existing ones, since the latter are just as likely as the former to be unable to pay; in fact, recent experiences show that even the best export customers run into financial difficulties.

Therefore, your accounts people must check every order as soon as it is received, and the credit status of the customer in question must be determined before the order can be accepted or refused. The credit rating of customers overseas can be checked in many ways. Dun & Bradstreet, for example, have computerised records which enable them to check the credit rating of almost any company in the world. There are a number of companies in Britain who supply a similar service, as will the international branch of your bank. Moreover, if you deal with the Export Credits Guarantee Department (ECGD) as a means of obtaining credit insurance (explained more fully in Chapter 10) they will not allow you to ship goods to customers who, from their point of view, are bad risks. If you use a factoring company the same applies.

If you travel overseas you can obtain credit ratings on customers from their local banks. The commercial officers of the British Embassy or High Commission will give you some indication as to whether or not it is safe to deal with a particular company. Should you appoint a local commission agent, as suggested in Chapter 5, he should be instructed not to send you orders from customers he knows to be bad payers, and you may, by paying him more, have him take the credit risk by becoming a 'del credere' agent. Hence, he will need to be given the authority by you to negotiate payment terms. Or, if you appoint a local distributor, you will need to check his ability to pay for the stock he buys from you, these terms being set down in the agreement you make with him.

What a small business can achieve, perhaps more easily than a large one, is the close relationship needed between sales and credit control, because credit control is a form of sales weapon. How a customer pays can make all the difference between his buying or not. Credit control is not, as so often seems to be the case in a larger company, a debt collection service. You are investing in an export customer to some degree, and it is, I suggest, for both sales and accounts to decide what form that investment should take. The amount of such investment will have to be included in the price you charge, but this also depends on how the customer is asked to pay. Credit control is yet another example of the value of all the company being involved with export.

The importance of this attitude to credit control can best be shown by the fact that if you borrow money at 17 per cent, or use money that costs you that amount because you could earn that return by using it elsewhere, and you expect to make a contribution to revenue of 5 per cent, then if the customer is three months late paying, you will lose all that contribution. Any further delay and you make a negative contribution, or a loss. To put this another way, if you expect a contribution of 5 per cent, then a bad debt of £1000 means you must generate a further £20,000 of export business to recoup that loss.

I shall have more to say in Chapter 10 about contributions you may expect from export, but let me point out here that they will seldom be all that high, and that you will normally have to work on narrow margins. All the more reason, therefore, to ensure you obtain those margins in full, and ensure you make money from export. You cannot, therefore, afford to have anything but the closest system of credit control you can install, and look on it as a means of both selling and avoiding losses.

Methods of payment

Reverting to the various methods of payment outlined in Chapter 8, if you know little, or can find out nothing of value, about an export customer, you are fully justified in insisting on payment in advance. After all, once you have sent the goods with the documents the customer will get them, and there is little you can do to force payment. Should you be supplying goods on a contract, with some payment in advance, insist on promissory notes for the balance, avalised (ie guaranteed) by a reputable bank, which means you can discount them if you need the money quickly.

Since few customers will pay in advance, because of the lack of protection they have that the goods will be sent, and if you wish to make sure of payment, ask for a confirmed irrevocable documentary letter of credit. This gives you the security of knowing that, provided you carry out all the conditions laid down in the credit (and you may ask for the conditions to be altered if you do not agree with them), you will be paid when you deliver the documents to the confirming bank. For this reason, more than half of British exports are paid for by this means. You can calculate for how long you will be out of your money and allow for this in your export price.

Rather more difficult are those customers who do not wish to pay until they have received the goods, or even some time after they have them. If you ship by sea you can prevent a customer having the goods by instructing your bank to withhold delivery, by not handing over the bill of lading in the event of non-payment of the draft, or a refusal to accept the draft. But you then have two problems, one being what to do with the goods, and the other, how to avoid losing too much on the shipment.

You can solve these problems, first, by asking the bank to return the goods to you. But this will involve you in paying the return freight and insurance, and assuming the goods will reach you undamaged.

Your alternative is to ask the bank to sell the goods to another customer in that country. This will cost you money, assuming that another customer can be found. What happens so often is that the bank puts the goods up for auction. You do not have to be clever to guess who bids for them, at a lower

131

price — the customer who refused to pay your draft, who gets the goods at a substantial discount, and that is the end of your contribution to revenue.

As we shall see in Chapter 10, you can insure to some degree against non-payment of drafts, but not to the full amount, so never allow a customer to pay against a sight or term draft unless you know him well, and are reasonably sure he will pay on the due date. Always keep a record in credit control of all drafts drawn on export customers so that you know when the money is due and if anything is overdue. And be ruthless in following up any overdue payments, as well as refusing to accept any more business from that customer on those terms.

If you ship by air, road or rail you have no means of withholding delivery and you must rely even more on your customer paying the draft, should you draw on him, on the due date. This is also the case with any form of open account which, for a small company, is not to be recommended except in exceptional circumstances. Factoring is the way to deal with customers who insist on open account.

As you have seen, discounts are one way of bargaining with customers, being allowed only for those who are prepared to pay promptly, such discounts reflecting the cost of the money you are expecting. Hence, standard export prices seem to be useless, since they leave no room for manoeuvre, and must result in varying rates of contribution. Far better, I suggest, to ensure a minimum contribution and increase it if possible by negotiation on terms of payment, because any small business must be concerned with the maximum contribution it can squeeze out of export sales.

Foreign exchange

As we saw in the previous chapter, by whichever method an export customer pays you, he will be paying in his own currency, because that is all he has. So if you quote him in sterling, you leave him to take the risk that by the time he pays you, that sterling may cost him more than when he accepted your quotation. This means he may prefer you to quote him in his own currency, because then he knows exactly what he will have to pay. In such a case, you take the risk that, when you convert his currency into sterling, you may not receive as much as when you quoted him because the rate of exchange has gone against you. Of course, you might get more if the rate moved the other way, but you may well feel that you are an exporter, not an expert in rates of exchange, and not be prepared to take the risks involved.

Rates of exchange are published daily, and quote the average buying price of the day before (that is, the rate at which the customer *buys* from the bank). For example, if £1 equals $1.81, this means when you sell pounds and buy dollars you receive that amount of dollars. Your American customer would have to buy pounds to pay your account by selling dollars to his bank. He will pay a little more than $1.81 for £1. There are also *spot rates*, which are rates for deals concluded on the spot, and *forward rates*, for deals to be done at some time in the future. Forward rates are spot rates either at a premium, which means they will be lower than the spot rate, or at a discount which means they will be higher.

Forward rates will usually be quoted for up to six months ahead, and will vary according to whether the deal is to be made on a specific date or during a specific time, say during one or three months, in which case they are called options.

Your solution to the problem of a customer wishing for a quotation in his own currency, yet ensuring that whatever rate your quotation uses you will not receive less when he comes to pay you in sterling, is to make a forward contract to sell the foreign currency to your bank, either on a particular date or between certain dates on an option basis. The bank will in turn quote you the appropriate forward rate and guarantee on their side to pay you the equivalent in sterling at that forward rate, whatever the spot rate of the day happens to be. But remember that you must sell the currency as agreed, even if you have not received it, although you can now insure with ECGD (see pages 137-40 and Chapter 10) against your customer not sending you the foreign currency on time.

Being able to quote a customer this forward rate enables you to be certain of receiving the exact amount of sterling you wish, and removes any possibility of your losing, should the spot rate of the day be lower than it was when the quotation was made. Moreover, if the forward rate stands at a premium, you can offer your customer a more competitive price. For example, if the spot rate for Deutschmarks is 3.8450 and the forward rate 3.8038, on a £10,000 order you could quote DM 38,038 instead of DM 38,450, which would be a saving to the customer of DM 412, and perhaps enough to clinch the order. Alternatively, you can, when using forward rates at a premium, keep some of the extra amount yourself, as additional profit, and give the balance to your customer. So there is no problem with quoting customers in their own currencies, provided that there is a forward market in them. Many customers prefer to know what the goods will cost in their local currency and you should not only be prepared to quote accordingly, but actively encourage them to accept quotations in local currencies.

Should you, as a company, buy from overseas, remember that you can make similar contracts with your bank whereby you buy the foreign currency forward at the forward rate, and thus know exactly what your purchases will cost you in sterling. You thus eliminate any possibility of paying more than you had intended. It is true that this method prevents you profiting from favourable rates of exchange, but as a small company you are unlikely to be in a position to gamble.

Cash flow

Possibly the most important question a small business must ask, before it embarks on exporting, is whether it has adequate finances to do this, that is to say whether it has enough cash flow. To do this your first consideration is an examination of your costs of making, or buying, the goods. If you manufacture them, you have to pay the suppliers of the materials, as well as the labour involved. You must therefore estimate what production you will need for export, and at what times of the year.

You will then need to estimate what proportion of your fixed costs are to be attributed to export, which is seldom easy. But unless you opt for marginal selling, you must allow for some of the fixed costs or overheads of the company in your export costings. To these you then have to add any specific fixed costs which, you will recall, I suggested you call the actual budget you are prepared to spend on getting export business. Initially, your out-of-pocket expenses should be minimal, especially if you take advantage of the help given by the government, but a good deal of time will be involved, and this should be costed.

The costs of handling the transportation and documentation have to be taken into account, whether you do this yourself or use a freight forwarder. Today, something like £50 per consignment is spent on documentation etc, and this excludes the actual freight charges and insurance of the goods, which you take into account when you make your quotations.

You then add the cost of the money you use from the time you make a quotation until you actually receive payment from the customer overseas, and this will vary with each customer. There is finally the cost to you of obtaining payment, either by using the services of a factor or handling the work yourself.

You must be sure that you have enough finance to cover these costs, or can raise such finance on terms which you can meet.

You then set against these costs your estimate of revenue, remembering that a sale is not a sale until it is paid for. The longer you have to wait for your money from your customers overseas, the greater the strain on your cash flow. The more accounts receivable you have, the lower the return on your capital. As you have already seen, late payments can remove contributions to revenue, while bad debts can have exports running at a loss within a short time. So you must be firm with overseas customers about payment, and be prepared to refuse business if you are unsure if and when a customer will pay you.

The third factor in any cash flow problem is stocks, because the lower the stocks you carry the less cash you will need to finance exports. While you will not wish to antagonise customers with long delivery dates, you must make sure that you can sustain your stocks with the cash flow you have.

All these problems will be familiar to you in your existing domestic business, but I suggest you keep a separate set of figures for export, and that you monitor the results continually to see that exporting is contributing to the company's revenue, without placing any undue strain on its cash flow situation.

Monitoring results

There are, as you know, many ways by which results can be monitored, but in the case of exports, the most useful is perhaps the return you obtain on the capital employed. This requires you to calculate the total contribution to the company's revenue, and divide it by the capital used, expressing the result as a percentage.

	£
Total Export Sales	110,000
Less Cost of Export Sales	60,000
Gross Revenue	50,000
Less Fixed Costs	10,000
Contribution	40,000
Investment in Export	7,000
Accounts Receivable	12,000
Fixed Assets	2,000
	21,000

In the above case the return on capital would be:

$$\frac{40,000 \times 100}{21,000} = 19 \text{ per cent.}$$

Assuming you can borrow money at 15 per cent your net contribution would be 4 per cent, but with interest rates falling you might be able to reduce the cost of money to 12 per cent which would give you a return of 7 per cent. If you use company money, the cost to you will be what you could do with it elsewhere.

If you take the above calculations and alter the figure for Accounts Receivable to £4000, your return on capital goes up to 30 per cent, so you can see the importance of not having customers overseas owing you money, and the necessity for determining when a customer will pay at the same time as you fix the price he has to pay. Credit control is, as I have said, a sales weapon and in a small company accounts receivable must be watched as closely as sales.

There are many other ways by which results can be monitored, one I have found most useful being the ratio of turnover to capital. Suppose exports use £10,000 capital in one year. If this costs you 15 per cent, then you are paying £1500 for its use. But if you can turn it over twice in a year, then you only pay £1500 on £20,000 of capital, which is much cheaper for you.

Another useful check on solvency is the ratio of current assets to current liabilities. Here a reasonably safe ratio is reckoned to be 2:1 although you can work on a lower ratio without too many difficulties. A higher ratio is, however, indicative that you may not be using your liquid resources to the best advantage.

The key to export profitability lies in, first, being able to arrive at accurate figures for costs. This is much easier said than done, but in my experience small companies so often fail because they do not try to ascertain their costs, or guess at them, often with disastrous results. Second, profitability lies in pricing according to these costs, and allying pricing to payment, each customer being treated separately. Every enquiry and order received must be evaluated on this basis if a small company is to profit from exporting.

Raising finance for exports

While you may be able to use your existing financial resources to start exporting, it is likely that you will have to finance some or all of your exports from outside the company. In the short term this may be done in a number of ways but, before considering these, reference must be made to the Export Credits Guarantee Department (ECGD), which was set up by the UK government some 60 years ago and is the world's oldest and perhaps most experienced credit insurance organisation. It has two main functions, the first being to insure exporters against the risks of not being paid by their customers overseas. (This will be explained fully in Chapter 10.) The second function is not to provide finance for exports, because that is the job of the banks, export finance companies etc, but to provide guarantees direct to these companies, which will enable them to lend money to the exporter, often on advantageous terms.

There are several ways in which you as an exporter can raise money to finance your trade:

1. You may obtain an overdraft from your bank. But if you have an ECGD policy, as described in Chapter 10, you are more likely to be granted a loan, because the bank knows that the ECGD will pay if your overseas customers cannot, or will not, pay. So you are providing some security for the loan. Moreover, you will be granted a special rate of interest, the amount being decided by international agreement.
2. If your customer has agreed to pay you by a confirmed,

irrevocable letter of credit (as described in Chapter 8, page 115), while you have no need of ECGD cover, the letter of credit is in itself good security for a bank loan. And if you have a transferable credit, you can use this to pay your suppliers and also pay yourself, when the goods are shipped.

3. If your customer pays you by means of a term bill of exchange, as described in Chapter 8, you may discount this and obtain cash by selling it to a discount house. But if you have ECGD cover you will get a better deal because the discount house knows that if the customer cannot, or will not, honour the accepted bill, the ECGD will pay.

These methods are based on raising money in cases where you require short-term credit, ie for less than 180 days, because normally letters of credit and bills of exchange are used when the customer will pay within six months. Moreover, the benefits of an ECGD policy can always be assigned to a bank as collateral security. And this can now be done in respect of the whole policy, or for all transactions in specified countries, for all transactions with a named buyer, or for individual transactions with a named buyer, at no extra cost to you. So having an ECGD policy makes sense in two ways: one to make sure you are paid by an overseas customer, and the other because this enables you to raise money to finance your exports.

There are other kinds of supplier credit backed by the ECGD, but notice that the ECGD has now withdrawn its short-term comprehensive bill guarantees for goods sold on up to two years' credit, because it was making a loss on these transactions, while there are now a whole host of other ways of raising money on short-term deals from banks, finance houses and factoring companies.

But you may still obtain ECGD backing for goods sold on credit terms of over two years, and borrow the money from a bank or finance house. Of course, such lending bodies may well have their own arrangements with the ECGD, in which case you may not need the cover yourself, but can leave it to them to cover themselves, and you at the same time, with the ECGD.

The ECGD still operates a number of buyer credits, supported by what they call a *buyer credit guarantee*. This means the buyer usually pays the supplier between 15 and 20 per cent of the contract price out of his own pocket. But the balance is paid direct to the supplier by the bank through a loan made to the buyer, guaranteed by the ECGD and at preferential rates of interest. This supplier credit facility was originally designed for large capital goods contracts of a million pounds plus, but it has now been extended to cover the purchase of capital goods for as little as £20,000, which puts it within reach of many small businesses. The facility is called a *general purpose line of credit*.

You should ensure that your customers are aware of these and other buyer credits backed by the ECGD, because they may well help them to buy from you.

Another way of raising capital to finance exports is via the banks' own scheme, all banks having a number of these which they offer to their export customers. For example, the Midland Bank has a special scheme for its customers who are exporting in a small way, but who do not have an ECGD policy, and who deal on a bill of exchange basis with customers acceptable to the bank. The Midland will offer credit for up to six months, without recourse, subject to your handing over the shipping documents and the bills to the bank. They charge 1½ per cent over the base rate and will advance up to 90 per cent of the amount outstanding.

Remember if you use a factoring company to collect payment from customers, that the factor will usually advance some or all of the money outstanding, but this tends to be a more expensive way of raising money than the others I have outlined above. If you deal with confirming houses, explained in Chapter 5, remember that they will, in effect, help to finance your exports, because they pay you in sterling when you supply the goods. They thus remove any risk of non-payment, and usually attend to the shipping of the goods as well, which saves you a good deal of money.

Finally, on a more general note, you should investigate other ways of raising money such as the European Investment Bank (EIB) of the European Community, which has various schemes for helping small businesses, either with direct loans or with loans from banks. The National Westminster Bank, for example, offers loans for companies in manufacturing and tourism of up to eight years at a very reasonable rate of interest. So contact the Commission of the European Communities if you wish to raise money.

SITPRO

I have already referred to the high cost of export documentation, and while a small business starting to export will have to face this cost, as exports grow you should be aware that the Simplification of International Trade Procedures Board, known as SITPRO, offers an opportunity for the exporter to reduce documentation costs. The objective of this organisation, which was set up by the Department of Trade and Industry, is to simplify the procedures by which goods are sent overseas, and already some 3000 exporters and freight forwarders use their export documentation schemes.

The basis of the schemes is the use of a single master document, which contains all the information needed for any export shipment (see Chapters 7 and 8). Once this master document has been completed by the exporter, by using a series of simple plastic overlays and a copier or duplicator, all the various documents can then be run off. This saves constant re-typing of the information, since the documents in the system are all of a standard size and format, and the relevant information for each will appear in the right place. It also means that mistakes will not occur once the basic information has been set down and checked, mistakes which can cause both you and your customers overseas endless time and money to correct. As your exports grow, you should consult SITPRO, as a means of saving money.

Moreover, SITPRO are heavily involved with the use of computers for documentary procedures, and have materials to help with the training of staff in handling the documents used in an export shipment. There are other companies in this field, such as Alpha Computer Systems who, with their microcomputer, produce specialised software for exporters, including the use of SITPRO documents.

Making money

There is no sure-fire way of making money from exporting, but a good deal will depend on your ability to forecast revenue. If you have exported previously, a commonly used method of anticipating trends in revenue is to use 'Z charts'. These, as you may know, show monthly or weekly sales, monthly or weekly cumulative sales and moving annual totals. If you have no past experience, you can only ask potential customers, commission agents or distributors (if you have them) what they think is likely to happen, or draw on your own personal experiences.

At the same time much will depend on your ability to forecast costs, and hence, to be able to price realistically. If you spread the work of exporting throughout the company, you can keep these costs low as far as overheads or fixed costs are concerned. Thus your main concern will be the variable costs of producing the goods, but these will be directly related to quantities, so are more easily manageable.

You should then note that why so many companies have failed in exporting from a financial point of view is, first, that they have not had enough capital to finance their exports, which means being familiar with every way money can be raised. Second, they have had too high break-even points, which means that either their costing or their pricing has not been correct. Third, they had had too delicate a cash flow, which could not stand the strain of the export orders. If you watch these three points in particular, you are more likely to make money from export than if you concentrate too much on export marketing, and leave these major factors to take care of themselves.

Chapter 10

How Can I Guard Against Failure?

Any small business which becomes involved with exporting is bound to be at risk at some time, and since you cannot afford failures, it is only sensible to guard against them as far as possible. The first period of inevitable risk is when your goods are being transported to your customers overseas, and during that time are in danger of being lost or damaged.

Cargo insurance

This is a large subject and you would be well advised to consult a good marine insurance broker, who not only can arrange for your cargoes to be insured when they are sent overseas, but will explain all the implications of cargo insurance.

You should, however, know something of the basis of cargo insurance, starting with the fact that, although there is no law which says that cargo must be insured, the responsibility for seeing that the goods are insured rests with their owner. The terms of delivery on which you sell define who is the owner of the goods, so that in an FOB contract, for example, the exporter is the owner up to and until the goods pass over the side of the ship's rail. Thereafter the importer is responsible, as you have seen in Chapter 4, for paying for the freight and insuring the goods. In a CIF contract, however, the exporter is responsible for insuring the goods, as he is for paying for the freight.

In practice, goods are usually insured on a through basis, that is from the time they leave the exporter until they reach the importer. It is up to the importer to say, when he places the order, if he will insure them or if he wishes you to arrange the insurance on his behalf, and up to what degree the goods are to be insured. You must, therefore, always ask an importer what he wishes, should he not have said on his order. If he is paying by a documentary letter of credit, he will probably have specified the way the goods are to be insured as part of the conditions under which you will be paid.

142

Under the principle of insurable interest, remember you cannot insure any cargo in which you have no interest, but that in addition to your interest, your customer also has an interest as the eventual owner, and interest can be passed on to whoever becomes the owner. Moreover, the carriers or handlers of the goods will also, at some time, have an insurable interest in the goods, because they could suffer if the goods were to be lost or damaged while they were in their possession.

Under the principle of indemnity, you insure goods for a stated sum of money, known as the insurable value. This should be such that, in the event of the total loss of the goods, their owner, on being paid this insurable value, would be in exactly the same position as he would have been had the loss or damage not occurred. The insurable value these days is usually the CIF value of the goods plus 10 per cent of that value, the additional 10 per cent being a recompense for the cost of replacing the goods, or to cover the inconvenience of being without them. For a total loss (when the goods are totally lost or destroyed) you receive the full insurable value. For a partial loss, that is if some of the goods are lost or there is some damage, you receive a proportion of the insurable value. If the goods are so badly damaged that to repair them would cost more than their original value, this is known as a total constructive loss, and their full insurable value is recovered from the underwriters who, however, have a right to the remains of the original goods.

It is up to the owner of the goods to decide against which risks the goods are to be insured, and provided such risks are specific (ie they can be defined), virtually any risk can be covered with two main exceptions. First, you cannot insure against what is called inherent vice. That is damage which cannot be avoided from the nature of the goods, such as sugar attracting water or butter attracting smells. Second, you cannot insure any unlawful cargo, such as drugs (unless you have a licence to export or import them).

Cargo insurance is handled by underwriters at Lloyd's of London, or the major insurance companies. The types of insurance you can take out have been defined and simplified by the Institute of London Underwriters, who have produced what are called Institute Cargo Clauses A, B and C. Clause A is virtually an 'All Risks' clause (shown in Figure 10.1, pages 156-60), while Clauses B and C are basic cover, and only to be used when the goods are unlikely to suffer damage. All three exclude war risk and any damage from strikes, riots and civil commotions, which have to be specifically added. You can also add a whole host of special additional risks if you wish.

Insurance of goods sent by sea is covered by the Marine Insurance Act 1906, while for goods sent by air there are special air cargo clauses. The various conventions covering the conditions of carriage define the degree to which carriers are liable, and you should note that claims must be made within 60 days of the arrival of the ship or 30 days of the arrival of the aircraft. You should also at some time examine the exclusions to any cargo policy, quite clearly stated in Clauses A, B and C.

Premiums are not all that high, depending on the nature of the goods, their packing, destination and the risks against which they are insured, the premiums being on average £1 per cent of the insurable value.

There is a formula which will enable you to calculate the insurable value, which is as a rule the CIF cost plus 10 per cent of that total. This means that in the event of a total loss, not only is the cost of the goods recovered, but also the charge for both the freight and the insurance premium which has been paid.

Suppose the cost of the goods to be insured is £180.00, and the freight charges £43.50, which means the CFR cost is £223.50. Assuming the rate is £0.75 per cent, your task is to insure for the CFR plus insurance premium (the CIF) and an additional 10 per cent of that total.

The formula is as follows:

$$\left(100\% \text{ of CFR} + 0.0075 \times \frac{110}{100} \text{ of CFR}\right) \times \frac{110}{100}$$

If you work out the above you will arrive at:

$$(100\% \text{ of CFR} + 0.00825\% \text{ of CFR}) \times 1.1$$
$$= (1.0825 \times £223.50) \times 1.1$$
$$= £247.88 \text{ or say } £248.00$$

Your insurance premium will be £0.75 per cent of the total insured value which we say will be £248.00, so the premium payable will be £1.86. Add this to the CFR of £223.50 and you arrive at a CIF of £225.16. Add 10 per cent to this figure and you get £247.68 or as near £248 as you wish. In fact, always make sure the total insurable value is over rather than under the

144

CIF, plus 10 per cent to ensure that you suffer no loss whatsoever if all the goods are totally lost, and it is customary to insure for a round figure, fractionally above the actual figure.

If you are a regular exporter, it would be impractical to take out a separate policy for each shipment so you can, under the principle of utmost good faith, take out some form of open cover or open policy. This means that Lloyd's, or the insurance company, agree to cover all your shipments, without being told in advance what they are, provided that you guarantee to advise them when the shipments are made. Under this arrangement, you will be allowed to issue your own insurance certificates, an example of one being shown in Figure 10.2 on page 161. Such certificates are part of the complete shipping documents, and by endorsing the certificate, claims may be made by the importer or anyone with an insurable interest in the goods.

Claims are made by having the loss or damage surveyed by Lloyd's or the insurance company, and sending this survey report, together with the relevant invoices, bill of lading or air waybill, and certificate of insurance, to the insurers, including a claim in writing against whichever carrier or handler you think caused the loss or damage. This helps the insurers to recover some of the loss they pay to you. Your broker will, of course, also handle claims, as well as negotiate the open cover for you. So one way to avoid risks of failure in export is to ensure that your goods are always fully insured against loss or damage in transit.

Credit insurance

You will doubtless be familiar with credit insurance from your domestic trade, whereby you can insure against loss due to your customers' inability to pay. To guard against failure when exporting, you must also insure against similar risks, which you may feel are likely to be more serious with overseas customers than those at home.

There are several companies who will do this type of insurance, the principal one so far as export is concerned being the Export Credits Guarantee Department, set up and financed by the government, as explained in Chapter 9.

If you sell overseas on terms of payment which are either cash in advance, or by means of a confirmed irrevocable documentary letter of credit, both dealt with in Chapter 8, you will not need credit insurance, since you are assured of being paid, or you have already been paid. If, however, you accept an unconfirmed letter of credit, or you agree to being paid by any kind of draft or bill of exchange, or you deal on open account, you run the risk that your overseas customer may not be able to pay you because of circumstances beyond his control. The purpose of the ECGD is to insure you against loss in this event, which means the government will pay you, if your customer cannot.

The risks against which you can insure with the ECGD are, first, the insolvency of the buyer, and his inability to pay you within six months of payment being demanded. Second, there is always a risk that some action by governments may prevent the proceeds of sales being transferred from one country to another, which means that while your customer may pay, you cannot receive the proceeds because their transfer has been blocked. For example, for many years funds could not be transferred between Britain and Zimbabwe so exporters were unable to receive money for their sales to that country. There may be many reasons why money cannot be transferred from your customers' countries to Britain, such as war, riots, even acts of God, and this is a risk which, as a small business, you cannot afford to take. Where import licences are concerned, if these are suddenly cancelled it is unlikely that you will be paid, should you have already sent the goods.

All these risks will be covered by the ECGD if you take out a policy with them. They will prefer you to cover all your exports, or at least a major portion of them, since they do not allow you only to cover exports to high risk countries. They also require you to keep some reasonable interest in the transaction, so in the case of a buyer's insolvency, or if the loss occurs before the buyer has been asked to pay, they do not pay 100 per cent of the loss, but only 90 per cent. But where the loss occurs after the buyer has been invoiced, or drafts have been drawn on him, then 95 per cent of the loss will be paid (except under a specific services guarantee). Of course, no loss will be made good if you fail to comply with your customer's requirements, or you break any existing regulations relating to the performance of the contract with your customer. But you can see that, while you may lose some of your profit, you are unlikely to suffer a loss on any transaction where payment cannot be made, so you are protected against failure in this respect.

Almost all policies are negotiated individually with the ECGD and you should ask their Insurance Services Group, based in Cardiff, to draw one up to suit you. For regular exporters, the ECGD will negotiate some form of *comprehensive short-term guarantee*, which covers exports made during 12 months, where the terms of payment do not exceed 180 days. For this you will pay an annual premium, at present £100, and make a monthly declaration of all shipments, for which you pay an additional premium each month. You can obtain cover from the date of shipment, but by paying an additional premium you can be covered from the date of the contract.

Companies which do not export on a regular basis (and you may wish to consider this when you start exporting) can have a specific services guarantee. You pay a premium on each shipment, which will depend on the ECGD's assessment of the risks of non-payment, and the length of time the cover is to last.

Under both these policies, provided that you submit fully documented claims, and have complied both with their conditions and those of your customers, you will be paid, in the case of insolvency, immediately on proof of the insolvency. Where a customer defaults on payment you will be paid six months after the due date of payment. Where payment is prevented by some form of government action, you will be paid four months after the due date of payment, or four months from the completion date of the formalities for the transfer of funds. Claims for any other losses are paid four months after the occurrence of the loss. You must, of course, help the ECGD to recover any losses and such recoveries would be shared by them with you.

There are numerous other types of policy available covering the provision of services rather than goods, royalties from licensing agreements and major contracts which may include the provision of both goods and services, as well as a new supplier credit financing facility which covers exports sold on extended credit terms, all available from ECGD in London.

Premiums are not all that high and should be counted as part of your costs when fixing a price. This may suggest to you the possibility of a higher price for high risk countries. But do not dismiss credit insurance because you export only to countries which you do not think are likely to block the transfer of funds to Britain. The problem with these sorts of risks is that they usually occur literally overnight, by which time it is too late. You must, as a small business, guard against that happening.

Personnel

It is to be hoped that so far this book has not made exporting sound too easy, because in practice it is more complicated in detail than might appear from what I have said. The point is that it can be learned, so all I have tried to do is to show the main considerations and areas with which you will be concerned, should you decide to extend or start your involvement with export. The best insurance against failure is, of course, the quality of the personnel you employ, and I have already suggested that initially you should not necessarily engage an export manager, or even special export personnel, because as a small company, you should involve everyone in export. You should encourage and help your staff to learn more about export than can be gleaned from a book of this kind.

One way of doing this is to let them attend the seminars being run by the Department of Trade and Industry. The DTI does not charge for these, and holds them all over the country, so contact the nearest regional office of the DTI to see if there are any seminars in your area.

The London Chamber of Commerce and Industry, as well as other Chambers of Commerce, runs frequent courses on various aspects of exporting, usually at no great cost. You should send some of your staff on them.

You must then encourage your key personnel to study for and pass the Institute of Export professional examinations. Many polytechnics and colleges of higher education run courses in the evening. Encourage junior staff and secretaries to take the Certificate in Export Office Practice, the CEOP, as this will give them a basic knowledge of shipping and the documents which they will have to use. For more senior staff there are Parts I and II, on completion of which they will be able to put MIEx (Grad) after their names, and claim a good all-round knowledge of exporting.

You should also encourage senior personnel to sit for the Institute of Marketing's Diploma in Marketing, since this will include the marketing side of export.

As regards languages, you cannot hope to be able to speak all the languages used by your customers, but you should encourage all your senior staff to learn at least one foreign language, the choice probably being between French, German and Spanish. A good deal depends on where your exports develop. If you find the Middle East is a good area for your small company, it would be useful if someone could learn some

Arabic, or for the Far East if you could acquire a smattering of Chinese. You may well conduct your business in English, but your customers will appreciate it if you can at least speak to them in their own language.

As your exports develop, you may well need an export manager. You should insist that he is a member of the Institute of Export, and you will find many qualified people advertising in the magazine *Export*. But even with an export manager, I suggest that a small company will still be more successful if it involves the whole company, so the export manager should be an integral part of the management team. The division of a company into 'home' and 'export' is, I suggest, not the best way for a small company to handle exporting, whatever may be the case in a large one.

You may well ask what special qualities export personnel should possess or acquire. Here let me suggest that they should have a basic knowledge of both simple economics and statistics. These are needed to understand the economies of countries overseas and your staff, therefore, are more likely to be able to spot opportunities, as well as avoid risks. You will have appreciated that success in exporting is dependent on the figures, because the margins are going to be slender. From personal experience I know that a good export manager or director will spend more time on figures than on selling, transport or any other activity.

Next I would rate an ability and willingness to learn as the mark of a good export person. When you travel overseas you need to be able to absorb information like a sponge, because you have to learn all you can about a country and its people in a short time. Since you will not be able to spend as much time travelling as you would like, you must make up for it by reading. You should read a quality paper such as the *Guardian*, and maybe the *Financial Times*. You should read the *Economist*, and then anything you can find which helps you to understand the world and the people in it. You should even learn while you are on holiday abroad. There are also many excellent books on various aspects of exporting, listed in Appendix 4.

You must understand the world and be able to get along with people of all races, religions, colours and nationalities. You must be something of a diplomat, and enjoy good old-fashioned trading, because that is what you will be doing, with people who are by tradition traders at heart. You must enjoy working in a highly competitive environment, because that is the character of the world market place.

Above all, you must employ personnel who are prepared to work non-social hours if necessary. Ships sail on holidays or at weekends. Visitors arrive from overseas at odd hours. Holidays overseas occur at different times, but whenever you have a holiday someone elsewhere in the world will be working and demanding attention. If you travel overseas, you will work a seven-day week, and as many hours in the day as you can manage without falling asleep. In a small business this attitude to work can be more easily fostered than in a large one and it can make, in my experience, for the best kind of exporter. In return, the job satisfaction will be high.

Legal aspects of export

Another way to avoid failure in exporting is not to become involved in legal disputes, either with your customers or with the people whose services you use. As a small business, you are unlikely to be involved with the law, provided you appreciate that there are laws governing all export activities, and you ensure that you do not break any of them.

It is not intended that you should become knowledgeable about all aspects of law, but there are certain areas of which you should be aware. In your domestic business you will doubtless know about the law of contract, and when exporting you will understand that you are making a series of contracts, first with your customers, second with your carriers, third with the underwriters insuring your goods, and fourth with the banks obtaining money for you.

International sales

There is as yet no law of contract applying universally to international sales, but instead of using the Sale of Goods Act 1979 where English law applies, you can base your contracts on the Uniform Laws on International Sales 1967, which incorporate the Uniform Laws on the International Sale of Goods, and you should, wherever possible, make contracts with your customers under these laws, unless they are prepared to accept them under English law. Basically, the duties of the seller are to deliver the goods called for in the contract, along with the necessary documents, and to transfer the goods to the buyer as agreed. The buyer must accept the goods delivered and pay the purchase price. Where you quote a buyer using one of the recognised terms of delivery, remember these have been codified by the International Chamber of Commerce under the term 'Incoterms', so add that word to your quotations to prevent any arguments about the precise meaning of the terms.

The latest version of 'Incoterms' is that of 1990. You may lay down any conditions of sale you please, but do not forget that a buyer's conditions of purchase take precedence over your conditions of sale.

International transportation

When you make a contract with a carrier you will do this under specific international conventions. These define clearly the duties of the carrier, what is to happen in the case of delays, deviations from the agreed route, misdelivery and payment of freight charges. Each convention requires the use of a special document and limits the liability of the carriers. As you know, shipment by sea usually requires the use of a bill of lading and is conducted under the Carriage of Goods by Sea Act 1971 (the Hague/Visby Rules). Shipment by air requires an air waybill and is under the Carriage of Goods by Air 1961 (Warsaw Rules). The CIM (Convention Internationale de Merchandises) covers shipments by rail, and the CMR (Convention de Merchandises per Routes) covers shipments by road. There is as yet no international convention for combined methods of transport, although the ICC have drawn up rules for guidance and a draft combined transport document.

International finance

If you use a bill of exchange as a means of obtaining payment from a customer overseas, remember there is a Bill of Exchange Act of 1882, and that the interpretation of this Act is now universally accepted according to the ICC's 'Uniform Rules for the Collection of Commercial Paper'.

Payment made by a documentary letter of credit is under the law of contract, but the ICC have interpreted the universal acceptance of the terms in their 'Uniform Customs and Practice for Documentary Credits' (1983). If payment is to be by open account, this will be subject to your conditions of sale. If you make a contract with your bank to buy or sell currency forward this will also be subject to the law of contract.

Cargo insurance
The contract you make with the underwriters to insure your goods will be under the Marine Insurance Acts of 1906 and 1909, although many of their provisions are now overridden by the various clauses of the Institute of London Underwriters.

Agents
If you appoint commission agents or distributors to act for you overseas the agreements will be subject to the law of agency. The same will apply if you appoint freight forwarders or a factoring company to act for you.

European Community law
As you know, Community law now takes precedence over English or Scottish law, and if you sell or appoint people to act for you in the EC you must do this in accordance with Community law.

Local laws
Your goods, when sold in other countries, will be subject to any local laws affecting their sale, and you should check to see that you are not breaking any of these laws before putting them on sale. This also applies to local regulations affecting the goods themselves, help being available here from the Technical Help for Exporters section of the British Standards Institution.

Never try to be your own lawyer in export, but always seek professional advice: it is the best way to avoid risks of failure. And do not fail to read the latest edition of *Law for the Small Business* by Patricia Clayton.

Marketing plans

Although I am not in favour of a small business spending much time on making grandiose export marketing plans, I do suggest that each year you should make out a brief plan showing basically what export results you aim to achieve, what this will cost the company and what contribution export will make to your revenue. There are as many ways of making a marketing plan as of skinning a cat, but one simple basis might be as follows.

Suppose you are a small company making and exporting hand tools. Your plan might read something like this. The objective is to export 5000 boxes of hand tools in 1990, to give a gross revenue of £100,000 and a contribution of £15,000. Always express an objective in quantifiable terms.

You then need a simple but reasonably detailed strategy as to how you plan to achieve your objective. Start with the countries where you intend to sell, and show how much each should contribute. For example, you might anticipate Kenya providing 40 per cent, Zambia and Malaysia 20 per cent each, and the balance from other countries in small amounts.

Identify your customers clearly, and in this case you might be selling to distributors in Kenya, Zambia and Malaysia, but to UK merchants and confirming houses for other countries. At the same time identify your users, who might be craftsmen and DIY specialists buying the tools from stores, supplied by the distributors and merchants.

Lay down maximum and minimum prices, and the terms on which you will supply. Specify the terms of payment and allow for the length of time you will be out of your money in your prices, as well as any credit insurance you think you will need.

Decide on what methods of transport you will use, and take into account what documents will be needed, along with what cargo insurance will have to be taken out.

Decide how much you are prepared to spend on obtaining these sales and how the money will be spent. For example, you might allocate £5000, use half of it for sales visits to your main markets, and spend the balance on advertising in a number of local publications (see Chapter 6).

Then make out your budget for the year, as follows:

Total Estimated Revenue

	£	£
Kenya	40,000	
Zambia	20,000	
Malaysia	20,000	
Others	20,000	100,000
Less: Cost of producing 5000 boxes of hand tools		75,000
Gross Revenue		25,000
Less: Promotion and Sales Costs		5,000
Net Contribution to Revenue		20,000

This would give you a return of 25 per cent on the capital employed, and allowing for the cost of money at 15 per cent, you would end up with 10 per cent net contribution.

The discipline of making a plan, and a budget such as this, means you can identify and decide what you propose to do about the two major aspects of exporting, namely the marketing of the goods or services overseas, and the finance you need for such sales.

You will notice in the budget above a net return, after allowing for the cost of money, of 10 per cent. In my experience, you will need to work on 5 to 10 per cent today, unless you are exporting goods which carry an unusually high margin of profit, which is unlikely. Margins average 7½ per cent, and any small business should be prepared to accept them, or stay out of export.

Conclusions

By now you should be able to decide, by answering the six questions asked in Chapter 1, whether or not your small business would be advised to become involved with export. Also, you ought to be able to work out some clear, quantified objectives for expanding your business into export, should you decide to go ahead. You will also appreciate that the unified European market to be created by 1992, when the Treaty of Rome is amended by the Single European Act, will almost certainly involve you in dealing with other countries in the Community, because they will be competing in your domestic market. So your only defence against the loss of existing business will be to compete in their markets. While you may argue that this will mean no more than expanding your existing domestic market, remember that you will be dealing in Europe with people who do not in the main speak English, who have different cultural backgrounds, and almost certainly different buying motivations from your domestic customers. The housewives of Calais and Dieppe may seem to buy much the same goods as those in Dover and Newhaven, but their buying motives and behaviour are in reality quite different, and these differences increase the further away you get from the Channel. Moreover, selling in Europe will inevitably involve you in transport, insurance, documentation, payment and customs problems which you do not face at home. So you will still need to know the export strategies as set out in this book.

You may, of course, decide not only to compete in some or all of the new Community markets, but also to tackle some countries outside Europe, depending on your resources and inclinations. But whichever you choose I suggest you bear in mind the following:

1. That there is a definite place in the Community, and outside it, for the small business, and that there is a great deal of help available to people who run small businesses.
2. That what is required today is the ability to adapt quickly to rapidly changing conditions, many being brought about by the development of satellite television, for example. So a new soap powder available in the USA today is known about and required in Japan tomorrow.
3. That the two most frequent requests from buyers are for quality goods and the service that goes with them, both requests being easily met by a small business.
4. That the best way to successful exporting is by involving the whole company in it, and not hiving it off to a few people working on their own. This will be especially important in dealing with the European Community.

In particular, if we are going to be Europeans from 1992 onwards, we might as well make the most of it. And if you handle business with people in other countries in Europe, or elsewhere, willingly and cheerfully, you will find that export can be a most rewarding and profitable operation, bringing with it, as I know from personal experience, great job satisfaction, as well as sound financial rewards.

INSTITUTE CARGO CLAUSES (A)
(for use only with the new marine policy form)

RISKS COVERED

1. This insurance covers all risks of loss of or damage to the subject-matter insured except as provided in Clauses 4, 5, 6 and 7 below.

2. This insurance covers general average and salvage charges, adjusted or determined according to the contract of affreightment and/or the governing law and practice, incurred to avoid or in connection with the avoidance of loss from any cause except those excluded in Clauses 4, 5, 6 and 7 or elsewhere in this insurance.

3. This insurance is extended to indemnify the Assured against such proportion of liability under the contract of affreightment 'Both to Blame Collision' Clause as is in respect of a loss recoverable hereunder. In the event of any claim by shipowners under the said Clause the Assured agree to notify the Underwriters who shall have the right, at their own cost and expense, to defend the Assured against such claim.

EXCLUSIONS

4. In no case shall this insurance cover

   4.1 loss damage or expense attributable to wilful misconduct of the Assured

   4.2 ordinary leakage, ordinary loss in weight or volume, or ordinary wear and tear of the subject-matter insured

   4.3 loss damage or expense caused by insufficiency or unsuitability of packing or preparation of the subject-matter insured (for the purpose of this Clause 4.3 'packing' shall be deemed to include stowage in a container or liftvan but only when such stowage is carried out prior to attachment of this insurance or by the Assured or their servants)

   4.4 loss damage or expense caused by inherent vice or nature of the subject-matter insured

   4.5 loss damage or expense proximately caused by delay, even though the delay be caused by a risk insured against (except expenses payable under Clause 2 above)

   4.6 loss damage or expense arising from insolvency or financial default of the owners managers charterers or operators of the vessel

4.7 loss damage or expense arising from the use of any weapon of war employing atomic or nuclear fission and/or fusion or other like reaction or radioactive force or matter.

5. 5.1 In no case shall this insurance cover loss damage or expense arising from

unseaworthiness of vessel or craft,
unfitness of vessel craft conveyance container or liftvan for the safe carriage of the subject-matter insured,

where the Assured or their servants are privy to such unseaworthiness or unfitness, at the time the subject-matter insured is loaded therein.

5.2 The Underwriters waive any breach of the implied warranties of seaworthiness of the ship and fitness of the ship to carry the subject-matter insured to destination, unless the Assured or their servants are privy to such unseaworthiness or unfitness.

6. In no case shall this insurance cover loss damage or expense caused by

6.1 war civil war revolution rebellion insurrection, or civil strife arising therefrom, or any hostile act by or against a belligerent power

6.2 capture seizure arrest restraint or detainment (piracy excepted), and the consequences thereof or any attempt thereat

6.3 derelict mines torpedoes bombs or other derelict weapons of war.

7. In no case shall this insurance cover loss damage or expense

7.1 caused by strikers, locked-out workmen, or persons taking part in labour disturbances, riots or civil commotions

7.2 resulting from strikes, lock-outs, labour disturbances, riots or civil commotions

7.3 caused by any terrorist or any person acting from a political motive.

DURATION

8. 8.1 This insurance attaches from the time the goods leave the warehouse or place of storage at the place named herein for the commencement of the transit, continues during the ordinary course of transit and terminates either

8.1.1 on delivery to the Consignees' or other final warehouse or place of storage at the destination named herein,

8.1.2   on delivery to any other warehouse or place of storage, whether prior to or at the destination named herein, which the Assured elect to use either

8.1.2.1   for storage other than in the ordinary course of transit or

8.1.2.2   for allocation or distribution,

or

8.1.3   on the expiry of 60 days after completion of discharge overside of the goods hereby insured from the oversea vessel at the final port of discharge,

whichever shall first occur.

8.2   If, after discharge overside from the oversea vessel at the final port of discharge, but prior to termination of this insurance, the goods are to be forwarded to a destination other than that to which they are insured hereunder, this insurance, whilst remaining subject to termination as provided for above, shall not extend beyond the commencement of transit to such other destination.

8.3   This insurance shall remain in force (subject to termination as provided for above and to the provisions of Clause 9 below) during delay beyond the control of the Assured, any deviation, forced discharge, reshipment or transhipment and during any variation of the adventure arising from the exercise of a liberty granted to shipowners or charterers under the contract of affreightment.

9. If owing to circumstances beyond the control of the Assured either the contract of carriage is terminated at a port or place other than the destination named therein or the transit is otherwise terminated before delivery of the goods as provided for in Clause 8 above, then this insurance shall also terminate *unless prompt notice is given to the Underwriters and continuation of cover is requested when the insurance shall remain in force*, subject to an additional premium *if required by the Underwriters*, either

9.1   until the goods are sold and delivered at such port or place, or, unless otherwise specially agreed, until the expiry of 60 days after arrival of the goods hereby insured at such port or place, whichever shall first occur,

or

9.2   if the goods are forwarded within the said period of 60 days (or any agreed extension thereof) to the destination named herein or to any other destination, until terminated in accordance with the provisions of Clause 8 above.

10. Where, after attachment of this insurance, the destination is changed by the Assured, *held covered at a premium and on conditions to be arranged subject to prompt notice being given to the Underwriters.*

CLAIMS

11. 11.1 In order to recover under this insurance the Assured must have an insurable interest in the subject-matter insured at the time of the loss.

11.2 Subject to 11.1 above, the Assured shall be entitled to recover for insured loss occurring during the period covered by this insurance, notwithstanding that the loss occurred before the contract of insurance was concluded, unless the Assured were aware of the loss and the Underwriters were not.

12. Where, as a result of the operation of a risk covered by this insurance, the insured transit is terminated at a port or place other than that to which the subject-matter is covered under this insurance, the Underwriters will reimburse the Assured for any extra charges properly and reasonably incurred in unloading storing and forwarding the subject-matter to the destination to which it is insured hereunder.

This Clause 12, which does not apply to general average or salvage charges, shall be subject to the exclusions contained in Clauses 4, 5, 6 and 7 above, and shall not include charges arising from the fault negligence insolvency or financial default of the Assured or their servants.

13. No claim for Constructive Total Loss shall be recoverable hereunder unless the subject-matter insured is reasonably abandoned either on account of its actual total loss appearing to be unavoidable or because the cost of recovering, reconditioning and forwarding the subject-matter to the destination to which it is insured would exceed its value on arrival.

14. 14.1 If any Increased Value insurance is effected by the Assured on the cargo insured herein the agreed value of the cargo shall be deemed to be increased to the total amount insured under this insurance and all Increased Value insurances covering the loss, and liability under this insurance shall be in such proportion as the sum insured herein bears to such total amount insured.

In the event of claim the Assured shall provide the Underwriters with evidence of the amounts insured under all other insurances.

14.2 **Where this insurance is on Increased Value the following clause shall apply:**
The agreed value of the cargo shall be deemed to be equal to the total amount insured under the primary insurance and all Increased Value insurances covering the loss and effected on the cargo by the Assured, and liability under this insurance shall be in such proportion as the sum insured herein bears to such total amount insured.

In the event of claim the Assured shall provide the Underwriters with evidence of the amounts insured under all other insurances.

BENEFIT OF INSURANCE
15. This insurance shall not inure to the benefit of the carrier or other bailee.

MINIMISING LOSSES
16. It is the duty of the Assured and their servants and agents in respect of loss recoverable hereunder

16.1   to take such measures as may be reasonable for the purpose of averting or minimising such loss, and

16.2   to ensure that all rights against carriers, bailees or other third parties are properly preserved and exercised

and the Underwriters will, in addition to any loss recoverable hereunder, reimburse the Assured for any charges properly and reasonably incurred in pursuance of these duties.

17. Measures taken by the Assured or the Underwriters with the object of saving, protecting or recovering the subject-matter insured shall not be considered as a waiver or acceptance of abandonment or otherwise prejudice the rights of either party.

AVOIDANCE OF DELAY
18. It is a condition of this insurance that the Assured shall act with reasonable despatch in all circumstances within their control.

LAW AND PRACTICE
19. This insurance is subject to English law and practice.

NOTE: *It is necessary for the Assured when they become aware of an event which is 'held covered' under this insurance to give prompt notice to the underwriters and the right to such cover is dependent upon compliance with this obligation.*

Figure 10.1 *Institute cargo clauses (A)*

SPECIMEN INSURANCE CERTIFICATE (Clients names are fictitious)

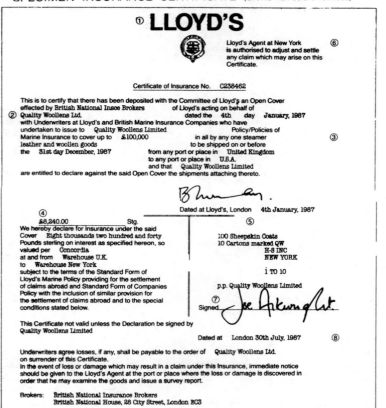

① **LLOYD'S**

⑥ Lloyd's Agent at New York is authorised to adjust and settle any claim which may arise on this Certificate.

Certificate of Insurance No.   C238462

This is to certify that there has been deposited with the Committee of Lloyd's an Open Cover effected by British National Insce Brokers   of Lloyd's acting on behalf of
② Quality Woollens Ltd.   dated the   4th   day   January, 1987
with Underwriters at Lloyd's and British Marine Insurance Companies who have
undertaken to issue to   Quality Woollens Limited   Policy/Policies of
Marine Insurance to cover up to   £100,000   in all by any one steamer   ③
leather and woollen goods   to be shipped on or before
the   31st day December, 1987   from any port or place in   United Kingdom
                                       to any port or place in   U.S.A.
                                       and that   Quality Woollens Limited
are entitled to declare against the said Open Cover the shipments attaching thereto.

Dated at Lloyd's, London   4th January, 1987

④
£8,240.00   Stg.
We hereby declare for Insurance under the said
Cover   Eight thousands two hundred and forty
Pounds sterling on interest as specified hereon, so
valued per   Concordia
at and from   Warehouse U.K.
to   Warehouse New York
subject to the terms of the Standard Form of
Lloyd's Marine Policy providing for the settlement
of claims abroad and Standard Form of Companies
Policy with the inclusion of similar provision for
the settlement of claims abroad and to the special
conditions stated below.

⑤
100 Sheepskin Coats
10 Cartons marked QW
                    H-S INC
                    NEW YORK

1 TO 10

p.p. Quality Woollens Limited

⑦
Signed

This Certificate not valid unless the Declaration be signed by
Quality Woollens Limited

Dated at   London 30th July, 1987   ⑧

Underwriters agree losses, if any, shall be payable to the order of   Quality Woollens Ltd.
on surrender of this Certificate.
In the event of loss or damage which may result in a claim under this Insurance, immediate notice
should be given to the Lloyd's Agent at the port or place where the loss or damage is discovered in
order that he may examine the goods and issue a survey report.

Brokers: British National Insurance Brokers
            British National House, 28 City Street, London EC3

INSURANCE CERTIFICATE

The Documentary Credit will indicate what insurance cover is required
and will call for either an insurance policy or insurance certificate.

Regular exporters, as in the specimen, normally arrange an open
contract to cover all exports during a specific period. This provides
insurance cover at all times within the agreed terms and avoids
having to obtain separate cover and a new policy for each shipment.

Insurance documents normally show the following details (numbers
correspond to those in the example)
1   The name and signature of the insurer

2. The name of the assured
3. A description of the risks covered
4. The sum or sums insured expressed in the same currency as that
    of the credit
5. A description of the consignment
6. The place where claims are payable together with details of the
    agent to whom claims may be directed
7. The declaration of the assured
8. The date of issue. This must be the same or earlier than the date
    of the document evidencing despatch except where warehouse to
    warehouse cover is indicated

Figure 10.2 *Insurance certificate*

Appendices

Appendix 1
Useful Addresses

National telephone dialling codes are given. Local codes may differ.

Alpha Computer Systems Ltd
Alpha House
12–27 Brunswick Place
London N1 6BR
071-250 1616

Association of British Chambers of Commerce
Sovereign House
212a Shaftesbury Avenue
London WC2H 8EW
071-240 5831

Association of British Factors
Moor House
London Wall
London EC2Y 5HE
071-638 4090

British Exporters Association
16 Dartmouth Street
London SW1H 9BL
071-222 5419

British Institute of Management
Management House
Cottingham Road
Corby
Northamptonshire NN17 1TT
0536 204222

British International Freight Association
Redfern House
Browells Lane
Feltham
Middlesex TW13 7EP
081-844 2266

British Standards Institution
(Technical Help for Exporters)
Linford Wood
Milton Keynes MK14 6LE
0908 220022

Central Office of Information
Hercules House
Westminster Bridge Road
London SE1 7DU
071-928 2345

Chartered Institute of Marketing
Moor Hall
Cookham
Maidenhead
Berkshire SL6 QH
06285 24922

Confederation of British Industry
Centre Point
103 New Oxford Street
London WC1A 1DU
071-379 7400

Croner Publications
Croner House
London Road
Kingston upon Thames
Surrey KT2 6SR
081-547 3333

Crown Agents
St Nicholas House
St Nicholas Road
Sutton
Surrey SM1 1EL
081-643 3311

Department of Trade and Industry
1 Victoria Street
London SW1H 0ET
071-215 7877

(Overseas Fairs and Outward Missions)
Dean Bradley House
52 Horseferry Road
London SW1P 2AG
071-212 0093/6277
Telex 297121

DTI Regional Offices:

Belfast
Industrial Development Board for
Northern Ireland
IDB House
64 Chichester Street
Belfast BT1 4JX
0232 233233
Telex 747025

Birmingham
West Midlands Regional Office
Ladywood House
Stephenson Street
Birmingham B2 4DT
021-632 4111
Telex 337919

Bristol
South West Regional Office
The Pithay
Bristol BS1 2PB
0272 272666
Telex 44214

Cardiff
Industrial Department
New Crown Building
Cathays Park
Cardiff CF1 3NQ
0222 825097
Telex 498228

Glasgow
Scottish Office Industry
Department
Alhambra House
45 Waterloo Street
Glasgow G2 6AT
041-248 2855
Telex 777883

Leeds
Yorkshire and Humberside
Regional Office
Priestley Office
Priestley House
Park Row
Leeds LS1 5LF
0532 443171
Telex 557925

London
South East Regional Office
Ebury Bridge House
Ebury Bridge Road
London SW1W 8QD
071-730 9678
Telex 297124

Manchester
North West Regional Office
Sunley Building
Piccadilly Plaza
Manchester M1 4BA
061-236 2171
Telex 667104

Newcastle upon Tyne
North Eastern Regional Office
Stanegate House
2 Groat Market
Newcastle upon Tyne NE1 1YN
091-232 4722
Telex 53178

Nottingham
East Midlands Regional Office
Severns House
20 Middle Pavement
Nottingham NG1 7DW
0602 506181
Telex 37143

(Export Licensing Branch)
Millbank Tower
Millbank
London SW1P 4QU
071-211 6611

Design Council
28 Haymarket
London SW1Y 4SU
071-839 8000

APPENDIX 1

EuroInfoCentres:

Birmingham
The European Business Centre
Chamber of Commerce, PO Box 360
75 Harborne Road
Birmingham B15 3DH
021-455 0268/021-454 6171

Glasgow
Centre for European Business
Information
(EuroInfoCentre)
25 Bothwell Street
Glasgow G2 6NR
041-221 0999

London
The Centre for European Business
Information
Small Firms Service
Ebury Bridge House
2–18 Ebury Bridge Road
London SW1W 8QD
071-730 8115 or dial 100 and ask for
Freefone Enterprise

Newcastle upon Tyne
North of England EuroInfoCentre
The Northern Development
Company
Bank House
Carliol Square
Newcastle upon Tyne NE1 6XE
091-261 5131

The Small Business Task Force
The Small Business Task Force
20 rue de la Loi
B-1049 Brussels
Belgium
(010 32 2) 235 05 38

**European Commission
Information Office**
8 Storey's Gate
London SW1P 3AT
071-222 8122

**Export Credits Guarantee
Department**
PO Box 272
Export House
50 Ludgate Hill
London EC4M 7AY
071-382 7000

ECGD Regional Offices:

Belfast
12th floor, Windsor House
9–15 Bedford Street
Belfast BT2 7EG
0232 231743

Birmingham
Colmore Centre
115 Colmore Row
Birmingham B3 3SB
021-233 1771

Bristol
1 Redcliffe Street
Bristol BS1 6NP
0272 299971

Cambridge
72–80 Hills Road
Cambridge CB2 1NJ
0223 68801

Cardiff
Welsh Office
Crown Buildings
Cathays Park
Cardiff CF1 3NQ
0222 824100

Croydon
Sunley House
4 Bedford Park
Croydon
Surrey CR9 4HL
081-680 5030

Glasgow
Berkeley House
285 Bath Street
Glasgow G2 4JL
041-332 8707

Leeds
West Riding House
67 Albion Street
Leeds LS1 5AA
0532 450631

Manchester
6th Floor, Townbury House
Blackfriars Street
Salford M3 5AL
061-834 8181

167

Hints to Exporters Unit
(Department of Trade and Industry)
Lime Grove
Eastcote
Middlesex HA4 8SG
081-866 8771

HM Customs and Excise
King's Beam House
Mark Lane
London EC3R 7HE
071-626 1515

Institute of Export
Export House
64 Clifton Street
London EC2A 4HB
071-247 9812

Institute of Patent Agents
Staple Inn Buildings
London WC1V 7PZ
071-405 9450

**Institute of Practitioners in
Advertising**
44 Belgrave Square
London SW1X 8QS
071-235 7020

Institute of Public Relations
Gate House
St John's Square
London EC1M 4DH
071-253 5151

Institute of Trade Mark Agents
69 Cannon Street
London EC4N 5AB
071-248 4444

**International Chamber of
Commerce**
(British National Committee)
Centre Point
103 New Oxford Street
London WC1A 1QB
071-240 5558

Investors in Industry (3i)
91 Waterloo Road
London SE1 8XP
071-928 7822

Licensing Executives Society
Registered office only:
33-4 Chancery Lane
London WC2A 1EW

**London Chamber of Commerce
and Industry**
69 Cannon Street
London EC4N 5AB
071-248 4444

**Paper and Board, Printing and
Packaging Industries Research
Association (PIRA)**
Randalls Road
Leatherhead
Surrey KT22 7RU
0372 376161

Road Haulage Association
Roadway House
35 Monument Hill
Weybridge
Surrey KT13 8RN
0932 841515

**Rural Development
Commission**
141 Castle Street
Salisbury
Wiltshire SP1 3TP
0722 336255

**Simplification of International
Trade Procedures Board
(SITPRO)**
Almack House
26-8 King Street
London SW1Y 6QW
071-930 0532

**Union of Independent
Companies**
71 Fleet Street
London EC4Y 1EU

United Nations
(London Information Centre)
14-15 Stratford Place
London W1N 9AF
071-629 6411

Chambers of Commerce Offering a Documentation Service to Exporters

Aberdeen
Aberdeen Chamber of Commerce
15 Union Terrace
Aberdeen AB9 1HF
0224 641222
Telex 73315

Ashford, Kent
London Chamber Ashford Office
(Documentation only)
Ashford House
Tufton Centre
Ashford TN23 1YB
0233 39562

Ayr
Ayr Chamber of Commerce
12 Alloway Place
Ayr KA7 2AG
0292 264696

Barking
London Chamber Barking and Dagenham Office
(Documentation only)
20 Cambridge Road
Barking IG11 8NW
081-594 3195

Barking Chamber of Commerce and Industry
20 Cambridge Road
Barking IG11 8NW
081-594 3195

Barnsley
Barnsley and District Chamber of Commerce
12 Victoria Road
Barnsley S70 2BB
0226 283131
Fax 0226 204587

Belfast
Northern Ireland Chamber of Commerce and Industry
Chamber of Commerce House
22 Great Victoria Street
Belfast BT2 7BJ
0232 244113
Telex 747538

Birmingham
Birmingham Chamber of Industry and Commerce
75 Harborne Road
Birmingham B15 3DH
021-454 6171
Telex 338024

Blackburn
Blackburn and District Incorporated Chamber of Industry and Commerce
14 Richmond Terrace
Blackburn BB1 7BH
0254 664747
Telex 635165 Chacom G

Bolton
Bolton Chamber of Commerce and Industry
Silverwell House
Silverwell Street
Bolton BL1 1PX
0204 33896
Telex 635109 Chacom G

Boston
Boston and District Chamber of Commerce
31a Market Place
Boston PE21 6ET
0205 51144

Bradford
Bradford Chamber of Commerce
Commerce House
Cheapside
Bradford BD1 4JZ
0274 728166
Telex 51449

Brighton
Federation of Sussex Industries and Chamber of Commerce
Seven Dials Corner
Brighton BN1 3JS
0273 26282
Telex 87323

Bristol
Bristol Chamber of Commerce and Industry
16 Clifton Park
Bristol BS8 3BY
0272 737373
Telex 449752

Burton upon Trent
Burton upon Trent and District Chamber of Commerce and Industry
158 Derby Street
Burton upon Trent DE14 2NZ
0283 63761
Fax 0283 510753

Bury
Bury and District Chamber of Commerce
Lloyds Bank Chambers
4 Bolton Street
Bury BL9 0LQ
061-764 8640

Cambridge
Cambridge and District Chamber of Commerce and Industry
The Business Centre
Station Road, Histon
Cambridge CB4 4LF
022023 7414
Telex 817114

Cardiff
Cardiff Chamber of Commerce and Industry
101-8 The Exchange
Mount Stuart Square
Cardiff CF1 6RD
0222 481648
Telex 497492

Carlisle
Carlisle Chamber of Commerce
4 Brunswick Street
Carlisle CA1 1PD
0228 26288

Chatham
Medway and Cillingham Chamber of Commerce
149 New Road
Chatham ME4 4PT
0634 830001
Telex 966272

Chester
Chester and North Wales Chamber of Commerce
6 Hunter Street
Chester CH1 2AU
0244 311704
Fax 0244 44535

Chesterfield
Chesterfield and North Derbyshire Chamber of Commerce
Commerce Centre
Marsden Street
Chesterfield S40 1JY
0246 203456

Colchester
Colchester and District Chamber of Trade and Commerce
1-2 High Street
Colchester CO1 1DA
0206 65277
Telex 987562

Coventry
Coventry Chamber of Commerce and Industry
123 St Nicholas Street
Coventry CV1 4FD
0203 633000
Telex 311033

Crawley
London Chamber Southern Area and Gatwick Airport Office
(Documentation only)
13a The Broadway
Crawley RH10 1DX
0293 30017

Croydon
Croydon Chamber of Commerce and Industry
Commerce House
21 Scarbrook Road
Croydon CR9 6HY
081-681 2165
Telex 8811136

Derby
Derby and Derbyshire Chamber of Commerce and Industry
4 Vernon Street
Derby DE1 1FR
0332 47031
Telex 377106

Doncaster
Doncaster Chamber of Commerce
50 Christchurch Road
Doncaster DN1 2QN
0302 341000

Douglas, Isle of Man
Isle of Man Chamber of Trade, Commerce and Industry
Royal Buildings
Parade Street
Douglas
0624 74941

Dover
Dover Chamber of Commerce
3 Waterloo Crescent
Dover CT16 1LA
0304 201388

Dudley
Dudley Chamber of Industry and Commerce
Falcon House
The Minories
Dudley DY2 8PG
0384 237653
Telex 336718

Dundee
Dundee and Tayside Chamber of Commerce and Industry
Chamber of Commerce Buildings
Panmure Street
Dundee DD1 1ED
0382 201122
Telex 76243

Edinburgh
Edinburgh Chamber of Commerce and Manufacture
3 Randolph Crescent
Edinburgh EH3 7UD
031-225 5851
Telex 72465

Exeter
Exeter and District Chamber of Commerce and Trade
Equitable Life House
31 Southernhay East
Exeter EX1 1NS
0392 36641
Telex 42603

Falkirk
Central Scotland Chamber of Commerce
Suite A, Haypark
Marchmont Avenue
Polmont FK2 0NZ
0324 716868
Telex 778583

Fareham
Fareham Chamber of Commerce
75 High Street
Fareham
Hampshire PO16 7BB
0329 822250

Glasgow
Glasgow Chamber of Commerce
30 George Square
Glasgow G2 1EQ
041-204 2121
Telex 777967

Goole
Goole and District Chamber of Commerce and Shipping
46 Aire Street
Goole DN14 5QE
0405 69164

171

Grantham
Grantham Chamber of Commerce
c/o Cole, Dickins & Hills
39 Westgate
Grantham NG31 6LY
0476 66661

Greenford
London Chamber Ealing Office
(Documentation only)
Unit 21
Derby Road
Metropolitan Centre
Greenford, Middlesex
081-575 3542

Greenock
Greenock Chamber of Commerce
14 Union Street
Greenock PA16 8JJ
0475 83678

Grimsby
Grimsby and Immingham Chamber of Commerce and Shipping
Yorkshire Bank Chambers
West St Mary's Gate
Grimsby DN31 1LA
0472 42981

Guernsey, CI
Guernsey Chamber of Commerce
States Arcade
Market Square
St Peter Port
Guernsey, CI
0481 27483
Telex 4191445

Guildford
Guildford and District Chamber of Commerce
Friary Mews
28 Commercial Road
Guildford
Surrey GU1 4SX
0483 37449
Fax 0483 571162

Halifax
Calderdale Chamber of Commerce and Industry
OP 66, Dean Clough Office Park
Halifax HX3 5AX
0422 365223

Hatfield
Hertfordshire Chamber of Commerce
Andre House
Salisbury Square
Hatfield AL9 5BH
07072 72771
Telex 25102

Hawick
South of Scotland Chamber of Commerce
19 Buccleuch Street
Hawick
Roxburghshire TD9 0HL
0450 72267

Huddersfield
Kirklees and Wakefield Chamber of Commerce and Industry
Commerce House
New North Road
Huddersfield HD1 5PJ
0484 26591
Telex 51458

Hull
Hull Incorporated Chamber of Commerce and Shipping
Samman House
Bowlalley Lane
Hull HU1 1XT
0482 24976

Inverness
Inverness and District Chamber of Commerce
13a Island Bank Road
Inverness IV2 4QN
0463 233570

Ipswich
Ipswich and Suffolk Chamber of Commerce and Shipping
Agriculture House
Foundation Street

Ipswich IP4 1BJ
0473 210611
Telex 987703

Isle of Wight
**Isle of Wight Chamber of
Commerce**
16a High Street
Newport PO30 1SS
0983 524390

Jersey, CI
**Jersey Chamber of Commerce
and Industry**
Chamber of Commerce Building
19 Royal Square
St Helier
Jersey, CI
0534 24536
Telex 4192341

Kendal
**Kendal and District
Incorporated Chamber of
Commerce**
PO Box 27
Exchange Chambers
10b Highgate
Kendal LA9 45X
0539 20049

Kidderminster
**Kidderminster and District
Chamber of Commerce**
Slingfield Mill
Pitts Lane
Kidderminster DY11 6YR
0562 515515
Telex 335672

King's Lynn
**King's Lynn Chamber of Trade
and Commerce**
17a Tuesday Market Place
King's Lynn PE30 1JN

Kirkcaldy
**Kirkcaldy and District Chamber
of Commerce**
17 Tolbooth Street
Kirkcaldy KY1 1RW
0592 201932

Kirkwall
**Kirkwall Chamber of
Commerce**
5 Main Street

Kirkwall
Orkney KW15 1RW
0856 2944

Lancaster
**Lancaster District Chamber of
Commerce, Trade and Industry**
St Leonard's House
St Leonardsgate
Lancaster LA1 1NN
0524 39467
Fax 0524 63280

Leeds
**Leeds Chamber of Commerce
and Industry**
Commerce House
2 St Alban's Place
Leeds LS2 8HZ
0532 430491
Telex 55293

Leicester
**Leicester and County Chamber
of Commerce and Industry**
4th Floor, York House
91 Granby Street
Leicester LE1 6EA
0533 551491
Telex 34694

Lincoln
Lincoln Chamber of Commerce
15–16 St Mary's Street
Lincoln LN5 7EQ
0522 23713

Liverpool
**Merseyside Chamber of
Commerce and Industry**
1 Old Hall Street
Liverpool L3 9HG
051-227 1234
Telex 627110/628702

London postal area
**London Chamber of Commerce
and Industry**
69 Cannon Street
London EC4N 5AB
071-248 4444
Telex 888941

London Chamber Cricklewood Office
(Documentation only)
1 Pond Row
Production Village
110 Cricklewood Lane
London NW2 2DS
081-450 3575

Westminster Chamber of Commerce
Mitre House
177 Regent Street
London W1R 8DJ
071-734 2851
Telex 268312

Lowestoft
Lowestoft Incorporated Chamber of Commerce
40 Gordon Road
Lowestoft NR32 1NL
0502 569383

Luton
Luton, Bedford and District Chamber of Commerce and Industry
Commerce House
Stuart Street
Luton LU1 5AU
0582 23456
Telex 825562

Manchester
Manchester Chamber of Commerce and Industry
56 Oxford Street
Manchester M60 7HJ
061-236 3210
Telex 667822

Middlesbrough
Teesside and District Chamber of Commerce and Industry
Commerce House
Exchange Square
Middlesbrough TS1 1DW
0642 230023
Telex 58232

Milton Keynes
Milton Keynes and District Chamber of Commerce and Industry
Silbury Court
384 Silbury Boulevard
Central Milton Keynes MK9 2HY
0908 662123
Telex 826932
Fax 0908 674958

Neath
Neath, Briton Ferry and District Chamber of Commerce
17 Elm Road
Briton Ferry
Neath SA11 2LY
0639 820269

Newark on Trent
Newark and District Chamber of Commerce and Industry
67 London Road
Newark on Trent NG24 1RZ
0636 640555

Newcastle upon Tyne
Tyne and Wear Chamber of Commerce and Industry
65 Quayside
Newcastle upon Tyne NE1 3DS
091-261 1142
Telex 53440

Newhaven
Newhaven and District Chamber of Commerce
24 Lee Way
Newhaven BN9 9SN
0273 513307

Newport, Gwent
Newport and Gwent Chamber of Commerce
Stelvio House
Bassaleg Road
Newport NP9 3EB
0633 256093
Fax 0633 213188

Northampton
**Northamptonshire Chamber of
Commerce and Industry**
65 The Avenue
Cliftonville
Northampton NN1 5BG
0604 22422
Telex 311165

Norwich
**Norwich and Norfolk Chamber
of Commerce and Industry**
112 Barrack Street
Norwich NR3 1UB
0603 625977
Telex 975247

Nottingham
**Nottingham Chamber of
Commerce and Industry**
395 Mansfield Road
Nottingham NG5 2DL
0602 624624
Telex 37605

Oldham
**Oldham and District
Incorporated Chamber of
Commerce**
8 Clydesdale Street
Oldham OL8 1BT
061-624 2482

Oxford
**Oxford and District Chamber of
Commerce**
30 Cornmarket Street
Oxford OX1 3EY
0865 792020

Paisley
**Paisley Chamber of Commerce
and Industry**
c/o McFadyen & Semple
6 Gilmour Street
Paisley PA1 1BZ
041-889 9291
Fax 041-841 1565
(Attention Paisley Chamber of
Commerce)

Perth
**Perthshire Chamber of
Commerce**
14-15 Tay Street
Perth PH1 5LQ
0738 37626

Peterborough
**Peterborough Chamber of
Commerce and Industry**
607 Lincoln Road
Peterborough PE1 3HA
0733 42658
Telex 32849

Plymouth
**Plymouth Chamber of
Commerce and Industry**
29 Looe Street
Plymouth PL4 0EE
0752 221151
Telex 45438

Poole
**Dorset Chamber of Commerce
and Industry**
Upton House
Upton Country Park
Poole BH17 7BJ
0202 682000
Telex 418297

Portsmouth
**South-East Hampshire Chamber
of Commerce and Industry**
27 Guildhall Walk
Portsmouth PO1 2RP
0705 294111

Port Talbot
**Port Talbot Chamber of
Commerce and Shipping**
Bryn Derw
141 Clasemont Road
Morriston
Swansea SA6 6AH
0792 771505

Preston
Central and West Lancashire Chamber of Commerce and Industry
2 Camden Place
Preston PR1 8BE
0772 555246/556261
Telex 677467

Reading
Reading and Central Berkshire Chamber of Commerce and Trade
43 West Street
Reading RG1 1AT
0734 595049
Telex 847423

Rochdale
Rochdale and District Chamber of Commerce
County Court Building
Town Hall Square
Rochdale OL16 1NF
0706 343810

Rugby
Rugby and District Chamber of Commerce
Temple Buildings
9 Railway Terrace
Rugby CV21 3EN
0788 544951
Telex 311794

Runcorn
Halton Chamber of Commerce
57–61 Church Street
Runcorn WA7 1LG
09285 60958

Scunthorpe
Scunthorpe, Glanford and Gainsborough Chamber of Commerce
58 Oswald Road
Scunthorpe DN15 7PQ
0724 842109

Sheffield
Sheffield Chamber of Commerce
Commerce House
33 Earl Street
Sheffield S1 3FX
0742 766667
Telex 547676

Shetland
Shetland Chamber of Commerce
122 Commercial Street
Lerwick ZE1 0HX
0595 4739

Slough
Thames-Chiltern Chamber of Commerce and Industry
2 Bath Road
Slough SL1 3SB
0753 77877
Telex 848314

Southampton
Southampton Chamber of Commerce
Bugle House
53 Bugle Street
Southampton SO9 4WP
0703 223541
Telex 47388

Stoke-on-Trent
North Staffordshire Chamber of Commerce and Industry
Commerce House
Festival Park
Stoke-on-Trent ST1 5BE
0782 202222
Telex 36250

Swansea
Swansea Chamber of Commerce and Shipping
Rooms F6/F7
Burrows Chambers
East Burrows Road
Swansea SA1 1RF
0792 653297

Telford
Shropshire Chamber of Industry and Commerce
Industry House
Halesfield 16
Telford TF7 4TA
0952 588766
Telex 35438

Tunbridge Wells
Royal Tunbridge Wells Chamber of Trade
10 Crescent Road
Tunbridge Wells TN1 2PD
0892 46888

Walsall
Walsall Chamber of Commerce and Industry
Chamber of Commerce House
Ward Street
Walsall WS1 2AG
0922 721777
Telex 338212

Warrington
Warrington Chamber of Commerce and Industry
9 Springfield Street
Warrington WA1 1BB
0925 35054

Westcliff-on-Sea
Southend-on-Sea and District Chamber of Commerce, Trade and Industry
845 London Road
Westcliff-on-Sea SS0 9SZ
0702 77090/78380
Telex 99450

Wigan
Wigan and District Incorporated Chamber of Commerce
25 Bridgeman Terrace
Wigan WN1 1TD
0942 496074

Wolverhampton
Wolverhampton Chamber of Commerce and Industry
Berrington Lodge
93 Tettenhall Road
Wolverhampton WV3 9PE
0902 26726
Telex 338490

Worcester
Worcester and Hereford Area Chamber of Commerce and Industry
Severn House
10 The Moors
Worcester WR1 3EE
0905 611611
Telex 335294

York
York Chamber of Commerce, Trade and Industry
c/o Joseph Terry & Sons
Bishopthorpe Road
York YO1 1YE
0904 629513

Overseas Chambers of Commerce in London

American Chamber of Commerce
75 Brook Street
London W1Y 2EB
071-493 0381
Fax 071-493 2394

Arab-British Chamber of Commerce
6 Belgrave Square
London SW1X 8PH
071-235 4363
Fax 071-245 6688

Australian-British Chamber of Commerce
615 Linen Hall, 6th Floor,
162–168 Regent Street
London W1R 5TB
071-439 0086
Telex 8954430

Belgo-Luxembourg Chamber of Commerce
6 John Street
London WC1N 2ES
071-831 3508
Fax 071-831 9151

Brazilian Chamber of Commerce
32 Green Street
London W1Y 3FD
071-499 0186

British-Soviet Chamber of Commerce
2 Lowndes Street
London SW1X 9ET
071-235 2423
Fax 071-235 3056

Canada-UK Chamber of Commerce
3 Lower Regent Street
London SW1Y 4NZ
071-930 7711
Fax 071-930 2012

French Chamber of Commerce
Knightsbridge House
197 Knightsbridge
London SW7 1RB
071-225 5250
Telex 269132

German Chamber of Industry and Commerce
12–13 Suffolk Street
London SW1Y 4HG
071-930 7251

Italian Chamber of Commerce
Walmar House
296 Regent Street
London W1R 6AE
071-637 3153
Telex 269096

Netherlands-British Chamber of Commerce
Dutch House
307–308 High Holborn
London WC1V 7LS
071-405 1358

New Zealand Chamber of Commerce
615 Linen Hall, 6th Floor
162–168 Regent Street
London W1R 5TB
071-439 0086

Norwegian Chamber of Commerce
Norway House
21-4 Cockspur Street
London SW1Y 5BN
071-930 0181

Portuguese Chamber of Commerce and Industry
New Bond Street House
1-5 New Bond Street
London W1Y 9PE
071-493 9973

Spanish Chamber of Commerce
·5 Cavendish Square
London W1M 0DP
071-637 9061
Telex 8811583

Swedish Trade Commissioner
172-73 Welbeck Street
London W1M 7HA
071-486 4545
Fax 071-935 5487

Turkish-British Chamber of Commerce and Industry
2nd Floor, Avon House
360-366 Oxford Street
London W1N 9HA
071-491 4636
Fax 071-493 5548

Yugoslav Economic Chambers
Crown House
143-147 Regent Street
London W1R 7LB
071-734 2581
Telex 21454

Further Reading

There are many helpful books about export, but the following is a selection of those likely to be most useful.

Conditions overseas

Hints to exporters is a series of small books, published by the DTI, giving essential details about each country. Constantly being up-dated.

Croner's Reference Book for Exporters is a loose-leaf book, up-dated monthly, which gives not only essential details about individual countries, but also the documentary requirements of each (Croner Publications).

Export marketing

International Marketing by Stanley J. Paliwoda (Heinemann) is a work of direct interest to all exporters.

International Marketing by L. S. Walsh (Macdonald & Evans) contains much helpful information about conditions overseas.

Marketing Plans by Malcolm McDonald (Heinemann).

Export practice

The Elements of Export Practice by Alan Branch (Chapman & Hall) is a basic guide to the techniques used in exporting.

Export finance

Raising Finance: A Guardian Guide, 3rd edition, by Clive Woodcock (Kogan Page); it shows how small companies can obtain finance.

Finance of International Trade by Alasdair Watson (Institute of Bankers), probably the most useful book on the various ways in which payment for exports can be made.

Thinking Managerially about Exports, a most helpful book written by G. Sharman (Institute of Export), which deals with management accounting in export.

Financial Management for the Small Business, 2nd edition, by Colin Barrow, (Kogan Page).

The law

Law for the Small Business, 7th edition, by Patrician Clayton (Kogan Page), deals with various aspects of law affecting the small business.

Legal Aspects of Export Sales and *Agency Agreements in the Export Trade* are two useful books, published by the Institute of Export, and written by Professor Clive Schmitthoff, dealing with export contracts and agreements made with representatives and agents overseas.

General

Distribution for the Small Business by Nicholas Mohr (Kogan Page) lists and describes all methods of despatch available, and compares them for cost, speed, safety and frequency. A chapter is dedicated to documentation.

Elements of Export Marketing/Management by Alan Branek (Chapman & Hall) is a useful companion volume to the same author's *Elements of Export Practice*.

Key Words in International Trade (International Chamber of Commerce) includes some useful definitions of words used internationally.

The Export Trade: Law and Practice of International Trade by Professor Clive Schmitthoff (Sweet & Maxwell) is a very comprehensive book on exporting and particularly strong on the legal side.

Economics and statistics

If you want to brush up your knowledge of these two subjects read *Statistics* by W. Harper and *'O' Level Economics* by L. B. Curzon, both published by Macdonald & Evans.

In addition to reading the quality daily press and the *Financial Times*, along with the *Economist*, there are certain publications which most companies find essential for exporting.

ABC Air Cargo Guide contains details of all scheduled air freight services from the UK.

Export is the journal of the Institute of Export, and useful for its articles on various aspects of export, job vacancies and jobs required.

Export Times, a publication particularly strong on various aspects of transport overseas.

Institute of Freight Forwarders Journal, useful for the various opportunities provided by members for the transport of goods overseas.

Lloyd's Loading List contains details of all sailings by ship from the UK.

You will find that most major banks, both in the UK and overseas, publish numerous leaflets and booklets mainly dealing with export finance, but also containing useful information about overseas countries. These are generally given free to exporters. The DTI also publishes a wall map distributed free to exporters from its regional offices.

Index

Figures in *italic* denote illustration; add. = address.